Jagdpanzer 38 Hetzer

Written by Hans-Heiri Stapfer

Walk Around®

Cover Art by Don Greer

Line Illustrations by Todd Sturgell

Squadron/Signal Publications

(Front Cover) German soldiers prepare an ambush in France, awaiting Allied armored columns penetrating into France during autumn 1944. The low profile was one of the advantages of the Jagdpanzer 38. The Hetzer proved to be a most unwelcomed surprise for Allied tanks operating on the Western Front.

(Back Cover) A Jagdpanzer 38 belonging to the 97. Jäger Division (97th Infantry Division) during retreats in Bohemia in Czechoslovakia in April 1945. This Hetzer carries a factory applied camouflage

About the Walk Around® Series

The Walk Around® series is about the details of specific military equipment using color and black-and-white archival and photographs of in-service, preserved, and restored equipment. *Walk Around®* titles are devoted to aircraft and military vehicles. These are picture books focus on operational equipment, not one-off or experimental subjects.

Squadron/Signal Walk Around® books feature the best surviving and restored historic aircraft and vehicles. Inevitably, the requirements of preservation, restoration, exhibit, and continued use may affect these examples in some details of paint and equipment. Authors strive to highlight any feature that departs from original specifications.

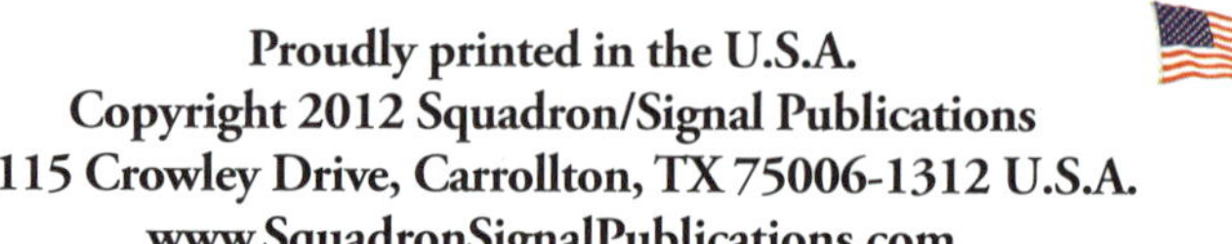

Proudly printed in the U.S.A.

1115 Crowley Drive, Carrollton, TX 75006-1312 U.S.A.
www.SquadronSignalPublications.com

Hardcover ISBN 978-0-89747-659-1
Softcover ISBN 978-0-89747-658-4

Military/Combat Photographs and Snapshots

If you have any photos of aircraft, armor, soldiers, or ships of any nation, particularly wartime snapshots, please share them with us and help make Squadron/Signal's books all the more interesting and complete in the future. Any photograph sent to us will be copied and returned. Electronic images are preferred. The donor will be fully credited for any photos used. Please send them to the address above.

(Title Page) This early-production Jagdpanzer 38 Hetzer is now part of the collection of foreign vehicles at the Armor Museum at Thun, Switzerland. This Jagdpanzer 38 is one of the few original Hetzer in the World that is now on exhibit in a museum. In all, 2,800 of these tank destroyers were built during World War II.

Acknowledgments

This book would not have been possible without the generous assistance of Dénes Bernad, Dr. Attila Bonhardt, Bundesarchiv (Swiss Federal Archives) at Berne, Deutsches Panzer Museum (German Armor Museum) at Munster, Rolf (+) and Alice Eigenmann, Vladimir Francev, Walter Grube, Kerstin Gutbrod, Adj Uof Martin Haudenschild, Walter Hodel, Christian Hug, Vladislav Krátký, Lehrverband Panzer und Artillerie of the Swiss Armed Forces, Panzer Museum at Thun, Switzerland, Wilfried Rorig and the Škoda Archives.

Introduction

By the end of World War II, the Jagdpanzer 38 Hetzer (tank destroyer type 38) had become the most widely used tank destroyer of the Wehrmacht (German army). Armed with the formidable Rheinmetall-Borsig Pak 39 L/48 7.5cm anti tank gun, the Jagdpanzer 38 was a highly efficient tank destroyer that served on the Western and Eastern fronts. Over 2,800 Jagdpanzer 38s were built between April 1944 and May 1945 – far more than any other German tank destroyer during Word War II.

The story of the Jagdpanzer 38 started in late November 1943, when a Royal Air Force bombing raid destroyed the Alkett factory at Berlin-Borsigwalde. Alkett was one of the main suppliers of the Sturmgeschütz III assault gun. The Oberkommando des Heeres (Army High Command) initially examined the transfer of the production of this assault gun to the Böhmisch-Mährische Maschinenfabriken AG (Bohemian-Moravian Machines Factory Limited) at Praha-Libeň, a suburb of Prague. Due to its geographical location, occupied Czechoslovakia was well outside of the range of Allied bombers. But the factory buildings of the Böhmisch-Mährische Maschinenfabriken AG (BMM) lacked the necessary lifting capacities to produce the 24-ton Sturmgeschütz III. BMM therfore proposed instead to develop a Leichter Panzerjäger (light tank destroyer) with a gross weight of only 13 tons. Reichskanzler (Reich Chancellor) Adolf Hitler personally accpeted this proposal on 6 December 1943.

Since the Red Army was fielding an enormous number of tanks on the Eastern Front, the production of a tank destroyer was a vital task. On 18 January 1944 – before the Hetzer had made it off the drawing board – a first order for 1,000 tank destroyers was placed, only to be increased to 2,000 vehicles shortly thereafter. Since BMM by itself could not handle such a huge quantity, the Skodawerke (Škoda works) at Pilsen (now Plzeň, Czech Republic) was chosen as a further contractor. The unit price of a single Hetzer was quoted with 54,000 Reichsmark.

The light tank destroyer was developed astonishingly fast. The chassis as well the automotive components were adopted from the well-proven PzKpfw 38(t) tank, which BMM built between May 1939 and June 1942. A wooden mockup was shown to representatives of the Heeres Waffenamt (Army Ordnance Department) in late January 1944. The first BMM-built Jagdpanzer 38 was ready for factory test trials on 1 April 1944, barely four months after the Wehrmacht had approved the design. The first Škoda-built Jagdpanzer 38s were accepted in July 1944. The first combat unit operating the Jagdpanzer 38 was the Heeres Panzer Jäger Abteilung 731 (731st Tank Destroyer Battalion) on the Eastern Front that received a total of 45 vehicles in July 1944. The Hetzer were not only issued to the tank destroyer battalions, but also in vast numbers to infantry divisions in order to create their own mobile tank destroyer force. The first unit to be equipped in the West was the 79. Infanterie Division, receiving its first 14 vehicles in August 1944, barely two months after the Allied invasion of Normandy. Aside from regular Wehrmacht units, the Hetzer also saw action with the Waffen SS.

One country allied to the Third Reich also operated the Jagdpanzer 38: Hungary. A total of 75 Hetzer were delivered to the Magyar Király Honvédség (Royal Hungarian Army) between December 1944 and February 1945. They were issued to four assault gun detachments and suffered heavy losses in action against the Red Army. A further 10 Hetzer were assigned in March 1945 to 1st Division of the Russian Liberation Army, a Wehrmacht formation fighting against the Red Army.

The first Jagdpanzer 38 (Fahrgestell-Nummer/chassis number 321 001) rolls out of the assembly hall of the Böhmisch-Mährische Maschinenfabriken AG (Bohemian-Moravian Machines Factory Limited) at Praha-Libeň on 1 April 1944. The first three production Hetzer had two tow hooks riveted on the lower front amor plate. These tow hooks were a direct take over from the PzKpfw 38(t), from which the Jagdpanzer 38 had adopted the automotive components. These tow hooks were deleted on the fourth Hetzer. The armored housing for the gun ball mount is attached the glacis with four screws on the left and three screws on the left – which is an unique arrangement for the first three Jagdpanzer 38. The first three Jagdpanzer 38 had a front drive sprocket with eight circular apertures cut in the outer sprocket. This type of front drive sprocket is a direct take over from the PzKpfw 38(t). All subsequent Hetzer lacked these eight circular apertures in the front drive sprocket. The first Jagdpanzer 38 ever built was painted in Dunkelgelb RAL 7028 (dark yellow) overall. (Vladimir Francev)

Since both Hetzer assembling plants were for a considerable part of World War II far outside the range of Allied bombers, production of the Jagdpanzer 38 ran rather smoothly until the last months of the war. Then the situation changed. The BMM factory at Praha-Libeň was targeted by some 400 B-17 Flying Fortresses and B-24 Liberators of the Italian-based 15th Air Force on 25 March 1945. A total of 375 tons of bombs were dropped on the plant during the 15th Air Force's last strategic mission of the war. The damage to the BMM factory was so severe, that production came to a halt. One month later on 25 April 1945, the British-based 8th Air Force targeted the Škoda factory at Plzeň. In their last mission of the war, 198 8th Air Force B-17 Gs dropped 526 tons of bombs on the Skodawerke, shutting down production until the German surrender.

This late-production Jagdpanzer 38 Hetzer was captured by Bulgarian troops fighting alongside the Red Army near Pécs in Southern Hungary during the winter 1944/45. No tactical number nor the Balkenkreuz (beam cross) – the German national marking – had been applied on the superstructure of the Hetzer. Vehicles built from November 1944 were equipped with an idler wheel containing six apertures. (Stephan Boshniakov)

The Swiss Army briefly evaluated one Jagdpanzer 38 in November 1945. The Hetzer had been modified with a horn on the left side of the glacis, just behind the license plate. A search light had been mounted on the left and right side. A Swiss Army license plate M-4086 ("M" stood for Militär/Army) has been mounted on the left glacis, just in front of the horn. (Swiss Army via Martin Haudenschild)

A Jagdpanzer 38 drives through Pécs in Southern Hungary. A large red star outlined in white has been applied on the glacis and both sides of the superstructue of this Hetzer, being operated by Bulgarian forces fighting alongside the Red Army. As a non-standard feature, this Hetzer is equipped with a Bosch blackout light located on the left fender, replacing the standard Notek blackout light. (Stephan Boshniakov)

The Swiss Hetzer (M-4086) lacks its Rheinmetall-Borsig Pak 39 L/48 cannon. The stamped license plate mounted on a platform on the glacis is a feature of the Swiss Hetzer. All G 13 had the license plate painted on the hull instead. This Hetzer was destroyed during shooting trials at the Swiss Army proving ground at Thun in the Berner Oberland Region in early 1946. (Swiss Army via Martin Haudenschild)

The assembling line of the Böhmisch-Mährische Maschinenfabriken AG (Bohemian-Moravian Machines Factory Limited) at Praha-Libeň was at full swing in late 1944. There were some 2,040 Jagdpanzer 38 built by BMM between April 1944 and March 1945. The production of the Hetzer at Praha-Libeň reached its peak in November 1944, when a total of 298 vehicles were built. Production in the BMM factory at Praha-Libeň came to a halt after a massive bombing raid on 25 March 1945. Some 400 Boeing B-17 G Flying Fortresses and Consolidated B-24 Liberators belonging to the Italian-based 15th Air Force targeted the plant with a total of 375 tons of bombs. All these Jagdpanzer 38 awaiting completion were painted with a red primer of Rotbraun RAL 8012 and lacked camouflage. However, the Notek blackout light mounted on the left glacis on some Jagdpanzer 38 were camouflaged in Dunkelgelb RAL 7028 (dark yellow). All these vehicles had a late type of periscope housing for the driver with a sheet metal rain guard, but were equipped with the early type of idler wheel with 12 small apertures and a perforated tool box mounded on the left fender. A top of the roof were three sockets welded to mount a folding jib-crane. All these Jagdpanzer 38 left the main assembling hall without the Rheinmetall-Borsig Pak 39 L/48 7.5cm anti tank gun, which was mounted later in the assembly process. The large aperture in the glacis caused by the missing gun was used by the workers to move the equipment into the hull of the Hetzer. (Škoda Archive via Vladislav Krátký)

Jagdpanzer 38 Hetzer (May 1944)

The first production examples of the Jagdpanzer 38 were equipped with the early 60mm-thick gun mantlet, which caused the first production examples to be nose heavy. The early Hetzer's idler wheel was adopted from the SdKfz 138 Grille (cricket), an artillery close-fire support platform for mechanized infantry units. There were a total of 12 small circular apertures in the outer idler wheel. Although a new type of idler wheel was introduced on the production line in August 1944, these early type of idler wheels were mounted on the Hetzer until the end of 1944. The early production example was equipped with a perforated toolbox located on the rear left fender.

Although a feature of early Hetzer, some perforated toolboxes continued to be mounted on the Hetzer throughout its production cycle. The early production Hetzer were equipped with a heat guard wrapped around the muffler.

Jagdpanzer 38 Hetzer (August 1944)

On the Jagdpanzer 38 built in August 1944 the original idler wheel with 12 small circular apertures was replaced by a modified idler wheel with only eight, but larger, circular apertures. Only limited numbers of the eight-aperture idler were actually mounted on the Hetzer, however. Meanwhile, the outer surfaces of the muzzle of the Pak 39 L/48 gun was threaded on Hetzer built until August 1944. A solid toolbox also replaced the perforated toolbox at that time.

The mesh heat guard was deleted from the muffler. The rim of each road wheel had a total of 32 bolts. A modified road wheel with only 16 bolts was introduced in September 1944. The arch shaped aperture in the lower portion of the cap that wrapped around the semi-elliptical leaf springs was mounted until mid August 1944. A rear-opening hatch for the commander had been introduced on the upper portion of the right rear armor plate. A hatch for the radiator filler was cut in the lower right armor plate of the rear engine bay in July 1944. From the beginning of the production until August 1944 brackets were welded on the inner surfaces of the protective skirts. A step was introduced on the lower right of the rear armor plate.

Jagdpanzer 38 Hetzer (September 1944)

Jagdpanzer 38 built in September1944 were equipped with a new designed gun mantlet, nicknamed Saukopf (sow's head), which reduced the weight by 200 kilograms. The thread was deleted from the muzzle of the Pak 39 L/48 gun. The road wheels were equipped with 16 bolts. The total 16 front leaf springs were increased in thickness from 7mm to 9mm, while the rear leaf springs remained unchanged. The arch-shaped aperture on the base of the cap that wrapped around the semi-elliptical leaf springs was deleted and in its place, a vertical stabilization rib was introduced on the cap. The front and rear end of the protective skirts were slightly bent in to prevent them being torn off when the vehicle brushed against trees. The brackets were riveted to the skirts. The hatch for the radiator filler located in the lower right armor plate of the engine bay received a horizontal welded handle. A top of the roof were three sockets welded to mount a folding jib-crane. The Jagdpanzer 38 built until late September 1944 had a square shaped rear cover plate for the track tension adjuster attached with four bolts on the housing of the idler wheel.

Jagdpanzer 38 Hetzer (May 1944)

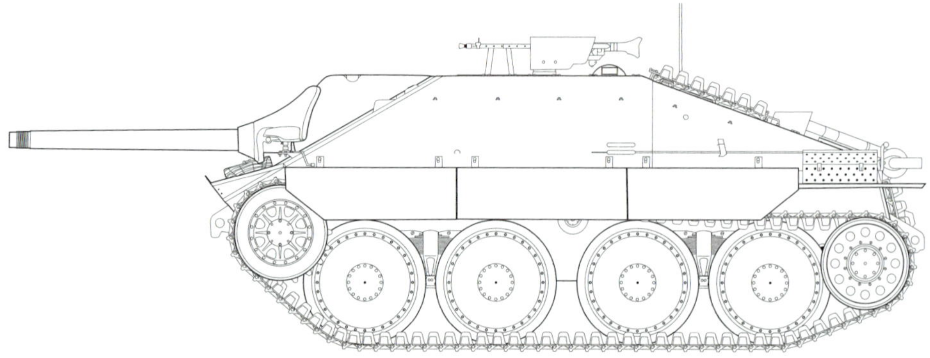

Jagdpanzer 38 Hetzer (August 1944)

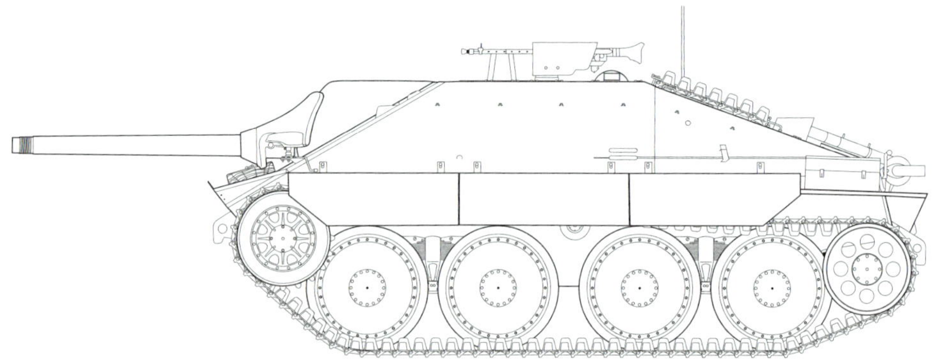

Jagdpanzer 38 Hetzer (September 1944)

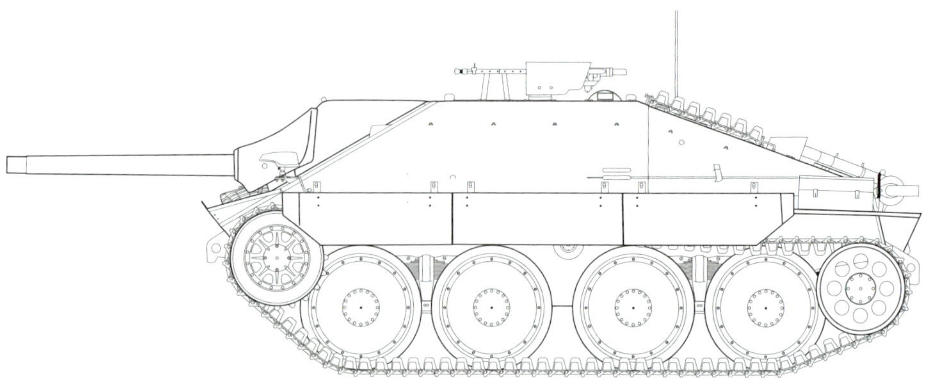

Jagdpanzer 38 Hetzer (October 1944)

A new periscope housing with a sheet metal guard was mounted on the Jagdpanzer 38 that left the assembly lines in October 1944. The periscopes were now mounted in apertures that were set into cutouts, making them flush with the front armor plate. Also in October 1944 a vertically mounted exhaust pipe with an integrated flame damper was introduced. The vertical exhaust pipe avoided trapping grenades, which might land on the engine deck. All Jagdpanzer 38 built by the Böhmisch-Mährische Maschinenfabriken AG (BMM) until the end of World War II had the flame damper mounted on the rear engine cover plate slanted to the right. The same flame damper configuration was used by Škoda until March 1945. The rim on the road wheel became thicker and rivets replaced the bolts holding the rim in position during the course of October 1944. The towing brackets in the front and rear of the extended armor hull sides were redesigned. Hetzer built in November 1944 had the ammunition supply for the Pak 39 L/48 7.5mm gun increased by five rounds to a total of 45 rounds. During December 1944 was an access hatch to fill the fuel tanks cut in the lower left armor plate of the engine bay. A handle was welded horizontally on the left hatch. The platform for the Notek convoy light mounted on the left bracket of the rear fender was deleted in December 1944 and the convoy light was mounted directly on the bracket for the rear fender. Jagdpanzer 38s built in November 1944 were equipped with a new idler wheel containing only six apertures. The BMM factory at Praha-Libeň continued to mount this type of idler wheel until the end of World War II. The housing for the idler wheel had been changed in shape and there was a triangle shaped rear cover plate for the track tension adjuster attached with three bolts on the housing of the idler wheel.

Jagdpanzer 38 Hetzer (October 1944)

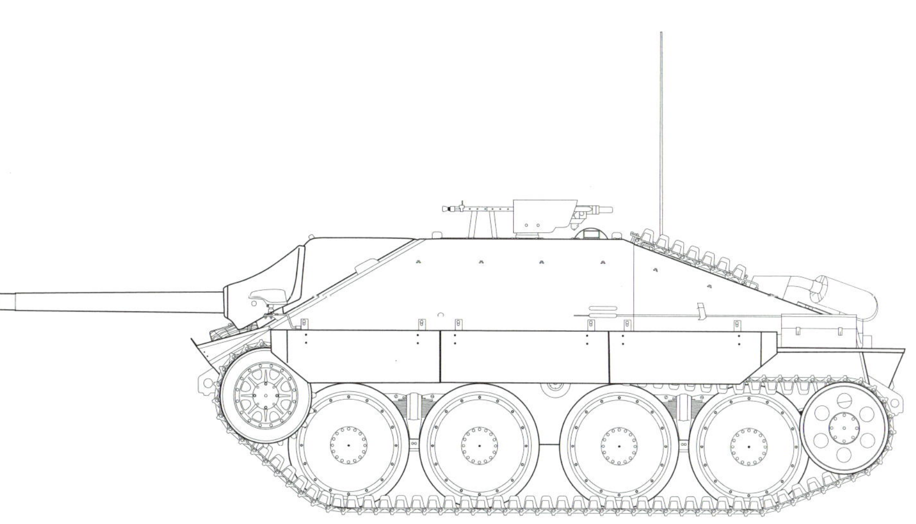

Jagdpanzer 38 Hetzer (April 1945)

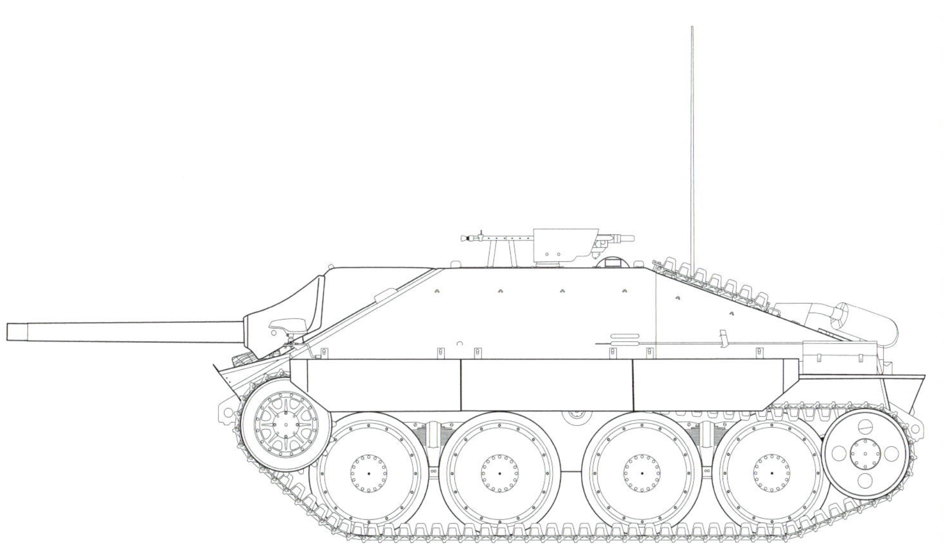

Jagdpanzer 38 Hetzer (April 1945)

The Hetzer received in early 1945 new track links with four diagonal ribs. The Jagdpanzer 38 built in April 1945 by Škoda at Pilsen were equipped with a modified idler wheel with only four apertures. Idler wheels with four apertures were a distinctive feature for Jagdpanzer 38s built by Skodawerke (Škoda works) and were never mounted on Hetzers manufactured by Böhmisch-Mährische Maschinenfabriken AG (Bohemian-Moravian Machines Factory Limited) at Praha-Libeň. Another distinctive feature for the late Škoda-produced Hetzer was the horizontal triangle shaped side support welded on the towing brackets on the front and the rear extended armor hull sides. These side supports were never applied on Jagdpanzer 38s built by BMM. The late production Jagdpanzer 38 built by Škoda had a provision to mount a shovel on the right rear engine cover plate with the means of a support made of sheet metal. No BMM built Hetzer had this provision. There were a number of Škoda built late production Hetzer that had just a single hinge mounted on the right access hatch of the lower rear engine bay armor plate. A further feature for Jagdpanzer 38s built in April 1945 by Škoda was the handle of the right access hatch, which was welded vertically and not horizontally as on previous models. BMM continued to weld the handle horizontally until the end of the war. Late production Jagdpanzer 38 built by Škoda had a straight mounted flame damper, replacing the slanted flame damper.

Škoda welded the brackets on their late production Hetzer against the inner surfaces of the protective skirts instead of riveting them, while BMM continued with the riveted variant until the end of the war.

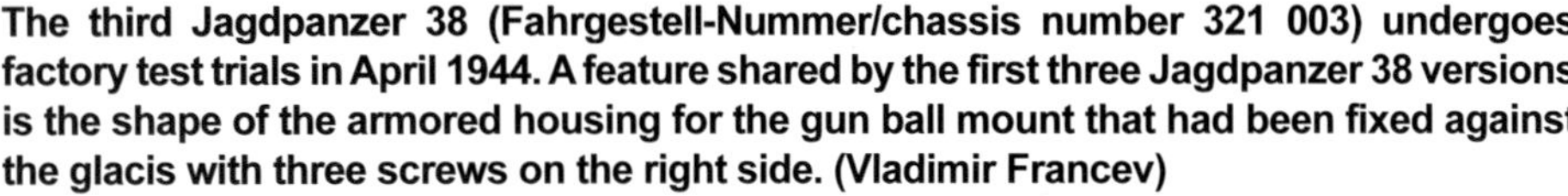

The third Jagdpanzer 38 (Fahrgestell-Nummer/chassis number 321 003) undergoes factory test trials in April 1944. A feature shared by the first three Jagdpanzer 38 versions is the shape of the armored housing for the gun ball mount that had been fixed against the glacis with three screws on the right side. (Vladimir Francev)

Final assembly is under way on these Jagdpanzer 38 vehicles in December 1944. The final drive casing is open on the Hetzer (Fahrgestell-Nummer/chassis number 321 683) in the foreground. The road wheels, the single return roller, as well the early type of idler wheel have already been mounted. (Vladimir Francev)

These factory-fresh Jagdpanzer 38s built in late 1944 by the Böhmisch-Mährische Maschinenfabriken AG (Bohemian-Moravian Machines Factory Limited) at Praha-Libeň still have the early idler wheel with 12 small apertures and the early horizontal muffler. (Škoda Archive via Vladislav Krátký)

Crewmen do maintainance on a well worn early-production Jagdpanzer 38 Hetzer during the street fighting on the Eastern Front. The perforated toolbox is a feature of early Hetzer. The absence of a tactical number on the superstructure is not too uncommon for the Hetzer. (Stephan Boshniakov)

The third Jagdpanzer 38 (Fahrgestell-Nummer/chassis number 321 003) built has the armored housing for the gun ball mount secured with four screws on the left and three screws on the right side. With the exception a single screw located on the upper part of the armored housing, all other screws were deleted on subsequent production models. The muzzle had been covered by fabric during the factory test trials. The third Hetzer built survived the war. (Vladimir Francev)

This factory fresh Jagdpanzer 38 built by BMM is equipped with the early 60mm thick gun mantlet. Hetzer vehicles built until August 1944 had a thread cut in the outer surfaces of the muzzle of the Pak 39 L/48 gun. This particular Hetzer's muzzle is covered by protective material. (Vladimir Francev)

Jagdpanzer 38 vehicles built in late August 1944 were equipped with a newly designed gun mantlet, nicknamed Saukopf (sow's head), which reduced the weight by 200 kilograms. The muzzle of the Pak 39 L/48 gun was not threaded but smooth, a feature that became standard on Jagdpanzer 38s that were delivered from September 1944 onward. This particular Jagdpanzer 38, built by Škoda at Pilsen (now Plzeň, Czech Republic), lacks the wooden jack base on the right fender. (Vladimir Francev)

This early production Jagdpanzer 38 (Fahrgestell-Nummer 321 042) has been equipped with the initial towing brackets in the extended armor hull sides. This type of towing bracket was mounted on Hetzers leaving the assembly lines up to October 1944. These towing brackets, which were weak and frequently broke during vehicle recovery, were a feature on the Jagdpanzer 38, since the PzKpfw 38(t) on which the Hetzer was developed, had two tow hooks, which were riveted toward the ends of the lower front armor plate. (Dénes Bernad)

Towing Lug

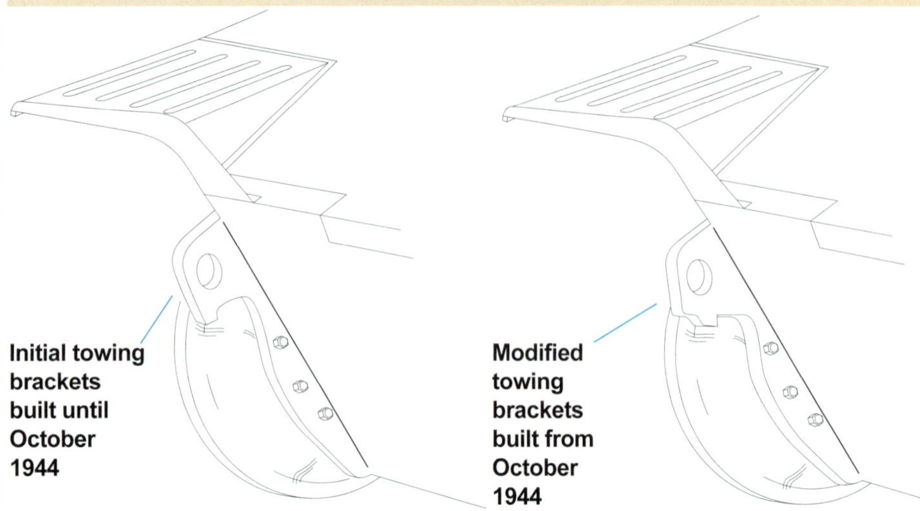

This type of a modified vertical towing bracket was introduced on the production line at BMM and Škoda in November 1944. However, the horizontal triangular side supports welded on the towing brackets were only introduced in April 1945 on Hetzers built by the Škoda factory at Pilsen. No such triangular side supports were ever welded on Jagdpanzer built by BMM at Praha-Libeň. This feature was subsequently adopted on all G 13 tank destroyers built for Switzerland. The triangular side support was welded only on the inner side of the towing bracket.

This is the outer vertical towing bracket of a late-production Jagdpanzer 38. These towing brackets replaced the different shaped examples of early-production models of the Hetzer.

This loop-shaped towing extension was welded as a field modification to the glacis of the Jagdpanzer 38 on exhibit at the Swiss Armor Museum at Thun. This loop-shaped towing extension was welded on after the original, weak towing bracket collapsed.

The vertical towing bracket collapsed on this particular Jagdpanzer 38 on exhibit at the Swiss Armor Museum at Thun, probably during an attempt to retrieve the vehicle from muddy terrain. Broken towing brackets were quite common on Hetzers during operation with the Wehrmacht. The poor design of the early towing brackets led to the introduction of towing brackets with a new shape in November 1944.

The lower armor plate is connected with the right side circular armor protector of the sprocket wheel cover. Three nuts secure the sprocket wheel cover to the armor plate. Compared with the PzKpfw 38(t) from which the Hetzer emerged, the arrangement has been simplified. The lower front armor plate was 60mm thick – 10mm thicker than the plate on the last production variants of the PzKpfw 38(t). The lower front armor plate is sloped at 40 degrees.

Unlike the PzKpfw 38(t), the Hetzer had a towing bracket rather than a tow hook on base of the lower front plate. On this particular Hetzer, however, the towing bracket is missing and has been replaced by a loop-shaped towing extension welded on the glacis as a field modification.

The left circular armor protector of the sprocket wheel cover of a Jagdpanzer 38 Hetzer is seen here from underneath.

A unique feature of the Jagdpanzer 38 is the jack base mounted on the vehicle's right fender. The jack base consists of a wooden block surrounded by three metal bands. No other armored vehicle of the German Wehrmacht ever had a jack base mounted on the fender.

The wooden jack base of the Jagdpanzer 38 is secured with a wing nut, allowing a quick removal.

The wooden jack base is seen here from the right side.

The left fender of the Jagdpanzer 38 Hetzer is bolted to the glacis.

A total of four longitudinal ridges were stamped into each left and right front fender to enhance the sturdiness of the metal. These fenders were manufactured of sheet metal.

The right fender of the Jagdpanzer 38 Hetzer on exhibit at the Armor Museum at Thun, Switzerland, is viewed from the front. Only the right fender had a provision to mount a wooden jack base. Rough front-line conditions frequently left the sheet metal fenders bent upward from impacts with obstacles.

Rivets hold the fenders to the Hetzer's superstructure, as seen in this view of the rear end of the left fender. Just behind the fender is the socket for the Notek blackout light, which is missing from this Hetzer on exhibit at the Swiss Armor Museum at Thun.

The Notek blackout light was mounted on the left glacis only, which was the driver's side. There was no blackout light mounted on the right side. The Jagdpanzer 38 Hetzer retained the Notek blackout light during its production cycle. Most other tanks and tank destroyers in the German Wehrmacht built in the second half of World War II were equipped with the more advanced Bosch blackout light instead. The light base on this Hetzer on exhibit at the Armor Museum at Munster is not accurate and is a postwar makeshift by the museum. The base on the Hetzer displayed at Thun (right) is authentic.

The covering of the Notek blackout light is viewed from the left. This covering cap was manufactured of stamped sheet metal. The Notek light was built in large quantities by the Nova Technik factory at Munich, Bavaria. The driver could regulate the light's intensity, which had a 40-meter (length) by 25-meter (width) visibility range.

The socket for the Notek blackout light is located on the left part of the glacis.

The initial driver's periscope was used from the start of the Jagdpanzer 38 production in April 1944 until September 1944. The driver had very limited vision with these prismatic periscopes and for proper driving needed the help of the commander. The driver's limited field of vision was regarded as one of the main disadvantages of the Hetzer. The protruding housing was a feature for the first variant of the driver's periscope housing. The glacis had a thickness of 60mm and sloped at an angle of 60 degrees. This particular Hetzer on exhibit at the Swiss Armor Museum at Thun has an astonishing mix of features from different generations. The early type of driver's periscope was phased out in September 1944, but mounted on this Hetzer are six aperture idler wheels that were not introduced on the production line before November 1944. By October 1944 the Jagdpanzer 38 had switched to the new type of driver's periscope with a rain guard.

Frontline experience showed that the initial design of the driver's periscope could allow the wounding or even killing of drivers when armor piercing shells penetrated into the crew compartment. Shells that struck the front plate below the periscope could skid up the plate, catch on the protruding housing, and then penetrate the vehicle.

These cast driver's periscopes were welded on the glacis of Jagdpanzer 38. (Walter Hodel)

Jagdpanzer 38s produced in October 1944 were equipped with a modified driver's periscope design that included a housing. The cast driver's periscope, a feature on early production variants, has been deleted. The periscopes were mounted in holes cut flush in the glacis. A sheet metal guard was added to prevent rain or sunlight from interfering with the driver's vision. This type of driver's periscope design remained unchanged until the end of the Hetzer production at the conclusion of World War II. The G 13 tank destroyer of the Swiss Army adopted the same driver's periscope configuration. This beautifully restored Jagdpanzer 38 on exhibit at the Deutsches Panzer Museum (German Armor Museum) at Munster in Northern Germany is in fact a rebuilt Panzerjäger G 13 (hull number 168) that saw service as M-78155 in the Swiss Army. It was the third from the last G 13 built at Plzeň and was delivered on 16 February 1950. The vehicle was donated by the Swiss Government to the Bundeswehr (German Army) in 1971 – two years before the last G 13s were phased out of service in Switzerland. The Kampftruppenschule 2 (Combat Training Unit 2) rebuilt the G 13 into a Jagdpanzer 38 Hetzer.

A sheet metal guard was initially mounted on the Jagdpanzer 38 in October 1944.

The sheet metal guard was welded on the glacis of the Jagdpanzer 38.

Final assembly of Jagdpanzer 38 is underway at the Böhmisch-Mährische Maschinenfabriken AG (Bohemian-Moravian Machines Factory Limited) at Praha-Libeň. These early Hetzer vehicles had a mantlet that was mounted on the production line between April and August 1944. The weight of the 60mm-thick gun mantlet caused the first production examples of the Hetzer to be nose heavy. Typically, the early-production models equipped with the heavy gun mantlet also had relatively small side pads. The early type of idler wheel with 12 small circular apertures cut in the outer wheel disc, were mounted on these Hetzer vehicles. There is a thread cut in the muzzles of the Pak 39 L/48 gun, as was common on the barrels of early-production Hetzer vehicles. (Vladimir Francev)

This factory fresh Jagdpanzer 38 was built by Böhmisch-Mährische Maschinenfabriken AG (Bohemian-Moravian Machines Factory Limited) in late August 1944. At that time a modified gun mantlet was introduced on the production line. Rheinmetall-Borsig, as the manufacturer of the Pak 39 L/48 gun, also discontinued cutting a thread into the muzzle. The thread was originally cut to accomodate a muzzle brake on the Pak 39/L48 gun. Muzzle brakes were screwed onto the muzzles of early-production examples of the Jagdpanzer IV L/48 tank destroyer. In contrast to this practice, however, no muzzle brakes were ever screwed onto the Pak 39 L/48 gun muzzle on any production Hetzer. When it was decided to abandon the muzzle brake from the Jagdpanzer IV L/48, Rheinmetall-Borsig discontinued cutting a thread in the gun. This Jagdpanzer 38 is equipped with a modified idler wheel with eight apertures. This kind of idler wheel was introduced in August 1944 and was mounted on a very limited number of Jagdpanzer 38. The so called Licht und Schatten (light and shadow) three-tone ambush camouflage was applied on this Hetzer on the production line. Colors applied were Dunkelgelb RAL 7028 (dark yellow), Olivgrün RAL 6003 (olive green), and Rotbraun RAL 8017 (red brown), which were the standard colors issued to vehicles of the German Wehrmacht during 1944. (Vladimir Francev)

On the early production models of the Jagdpanzer 38 only two bolts secure the gun ball mount's armored housing to the glacis. This circular plate holds in place the bearing of the vertical upper pivot pin of the cardan that holds the Rheinmetall-Borsig Pak 39 L/48 7.5cm cannon. The first production examples of the Jagdpanzer 38 were equipped with the early 60mm-thick gun mantlet that caused the first production examples to be nose heavy. This early type of gun mantlet was mounted on the Jagdpanzer 38 Hetzer from the start of the production in April 1944 until late August 1944, when the original gun mantlet was replaced by a new designed gun mantlet that weighed 200 kilogramms less. (Dénes Bernad)

The late type Saukopf gun mantlet was wider than the initial gun mantlet mounted on Hetzer and covered the gun carriage. Protruding elements with bolts for fixing the mantlet and the gun were eliminated on the armored housing for the gun ball mount introduced in late August 1944. The armored housing remained unchanged until the end of World War II. The circular plate in the top center of the gun mantlet has been modified, when compared to early-production models of the Hetzer. This particular Hetzer lacks the square block that was welded as a stop for the gun mantlet centerline on the armored housing for the gun ball mount. The stop block was welded on the gun mantlet of most Jagdpanzer 38 equipped with the late type Saukopf gun mantlet. (Walter Hodel)

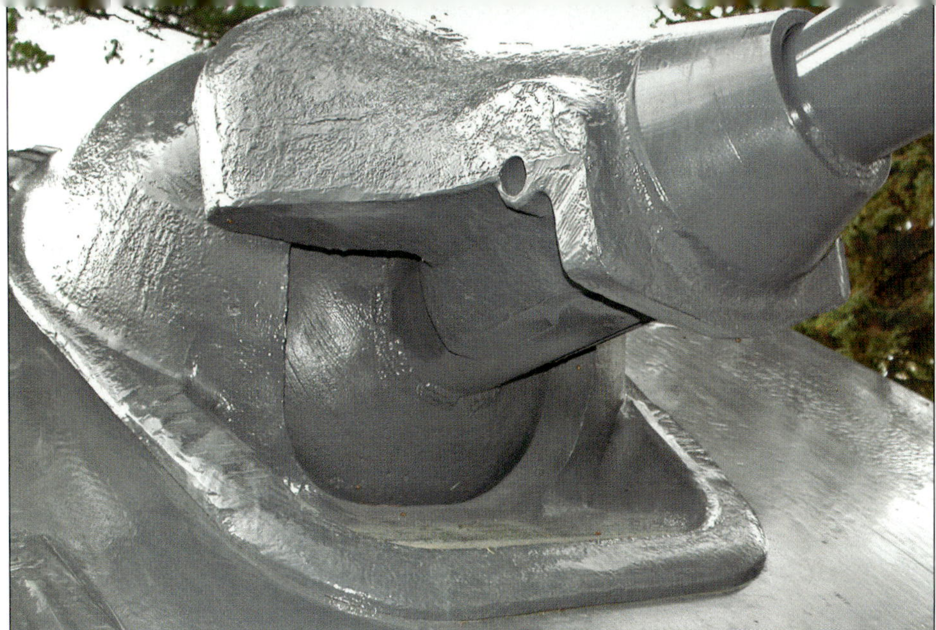

The initial, 60mm-thick gun mantlet of the Jagdpanzer 38 was mounted on vehicles on the production line between April and August 1944. (Dénes Bernad)

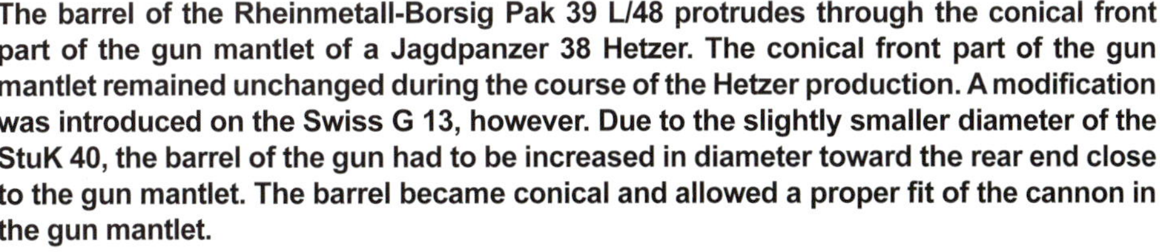

The barrel of the Rheinmetall-Borsig Pak 39 L/48 protrudes through the conical front part of the gun mantlet of a Jagdpanzer 38 Hetzer. The conical front part of the gun mantlet remained unchanged during the course of the Hetzer production. A modification was introduced on the Swiss G 13, however. Due to the slightly smaller diameter of the StuK 40, the barrel of the gun had to be increased in diameter toward the rear end close to the gun mantlet. The barrel became conical and allowed a proper fit of the cannon in the gun mantlet.

The so-called Saukopf (sow's head) gun mantlet, which weighed 200 kilograms less than its predecessor, was introduced on the production line in late August 1944.

None of the Rheinmetall-Borsig Pak 39 L/48 7.5cm guns that were mounted on all operational Jagdpanzer 38 Hetzer vehicles had a muzzle brake. Threading for a muzzle brake was cut in the exterior of the muzzles of Jagdpanzer 38 vehicles delivered until August 1944, but no muzzle brake was ever used. After August 1944, the threading was deleted and the end of gun became smooth, as on this particular Hetzer. The barrels' inner surface is rifled to put a spin on the shells it fires in order to increase targeting accuracy.

This Jagdpanzer 38 Hetzer “Black 132” became a victim of accurate Soviet anti tank fire in Eastern Hungary during autumn 1944. The tank destroyer is equipped with an early type of gun mantlet for the Rheinmetall-Borsig Pak 39 L/48 7.5cm gun and the outer muzzle surface features threading, which is a feature of early-production Hetzer vehicles. The square block welded to the top of the armored housing for the gun ball mount is the stop for the gun mantlet. This block was welded on a few Hetzer vehicles that were equipped with the early gun mantlet. This stop became standard on subsequent variants of the Hetzer that were equipped with the new Saukopf gun mantlet. Mounted on the right rear fender of this particular Hetzer is a non-standard trapzoidal wooden bin, which was fitted on a number of early Jagdpanzer 38 vehicles assigned to the Eastern Front. Standard production Hetzer vehicles had no such bin. A dedicated field modification was the rain guard mounted on top of the driver’s periscope housing. Enemy fire has blown off the right front protection skirt and the roof armor plate is also missing on this particular vehicle. This Jagdpanzer 38 has its tactical number “Black 132” outlined in white. A Balkenkreuz (beam cross) is located just below the tactical number on the superstructure. The majority of the Hetzer vehicles assigned to combat units displayed no tactical numbers or national markings. (Dénes Bernad Archives)

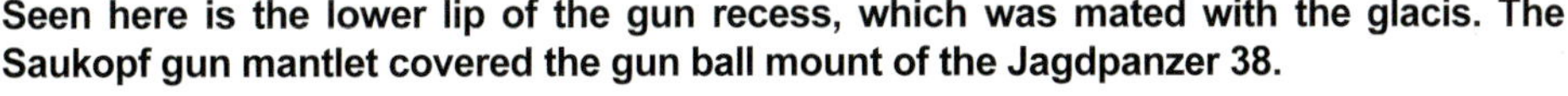

Seen here is the lower lip of the gun recess, which was mated with the glacis. The Saukopf gun mantlet covered the gun ball mount of the Jagdpanzer 38.

The extensions of the gun mantlet are welded on the barrel of the Pak 39 L/48 7.5cm gun.

This is the lower right part of the Saukopf gun mantlet. The firing height of the Pak 39 L/48 7.5cm gun was only 1.40 meters above ground level.

The Rheinmetall-Borsig Pak 39 L/48 7.5cm anti tank gun of the Jagdpanzer 38 Hetzer was secured in a mount supported by the upper hull plate.

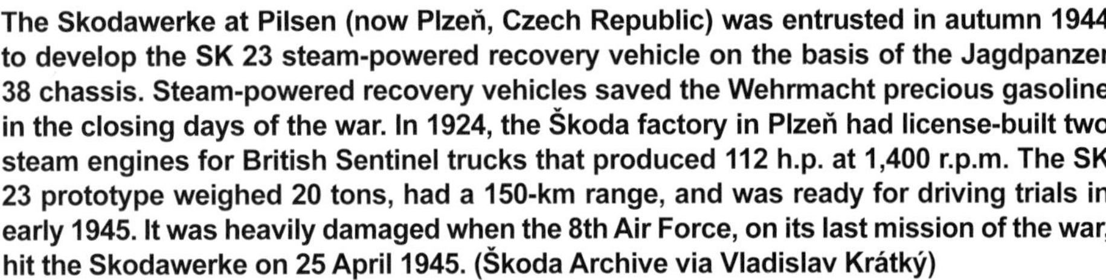

The Skodawerke at Pilsen (now Plzeň, Czech Republic) was entrusted in autumn 1944 to develop the SK 23 steam-powered recovery vehicle on the basis of the Jagdpanzer 38 chassis. Steam-powered recovery vehicles saved the Wehrmacht precious gasoline in the closing days of the war. In 1924, the Škoda factory in Plzeň had license-built two steam engines for British Sentinel trucks that produced 112 h.p. at 1,400 r.p.m. The SK 23 prototype weighed 20 tons, had a 150-km range, and was ready for driving trials in early 1945. It was heavily damaged when the 8th Air Force, on its last mission of the war, hit the Skodawerke on 25 April 1945. (Škoda Archive via Vladislav Krátký)

The third Jagdpanzer 38 (Fahrgestell-Nummer/chassis number 321 003) undergoes factory test trials at the Böhmisch-Mährische Maschinenfabriken AG (Bohemian-Moravian Machines Factory Limited) in April 1944. A temporary license plate has been attached to this vehicle's fender. (Vladimir Francev)

Böhmisch-Mährische Maschinenfabriken AG (Bohemian-Moravian Machines Factory Limited or "BMM") built this very early-production Jagdpanzer 38 at Praha-Libeň in May 1944. It features the early, 60mm-thick gun mantlet, the initial cast driver's periscope, and the original towing brackets in the front of the extended armor hull sides. Its protective side skirts are straight and flat rather then bent at the front and rear ends as later became standard. The vehicle carries a perforated toolbox on the rear left fender and a heat guard envelops the muffler. BMM delivered this Hetzer in Dunkelgelb RAL 7028 (dark yellow) overall. (Vladimir Francev)

The three colors in the factory-applied Licht und Schatten (light and shadow) ambush camouflage on this new Jagdpanzer 38 at BMM in Praha-Libeň in late August 1944 are standard for Wehrmacht vehicles in 1944: Dunkelgelb RAL 7028 (dark yellow), Olivgrün RAL 6003 (olive green), and Rotbraun RAL 8017 (red brown). (Vladimir Francev)

This factory-fresh Jagdpanzer 38, manufactured by Škoda at Pilsen (now Plzeň, Czech Republic), lacks the wooden jack base on the right fender and has no remote-controlled MG 34 machine gun mounted on top of the roof (although the V-shaped armor shield for the weapon has already been mounted). This Hetzer has a solid, rather than a perforated, tool box and is equipped with the early type of road wheel with of 32 bolts and an early type of idler wheel with 12 small apertures. The Licht und Schatten (light and shadow) ambush camouflage pattern applied to Jagdpanzer 38 vehicles built by Škoda was different from the pattern that BMM painted on its Hetzer vehicles. This particular Hetzer's camouflage features the standard colors of the German Wehrmacht: Dunkelgelb RAL 7028 (dark yellow), Olivgrün RAL 6003 (olive green) and Rotbraun RAL 8017 (red brown). The Hetzer was protected by 20mm side armor, sloped at an angle of 40 degrees. The hull was manufactured by the Komotauer Edelstahlhütte AG, the former Poldihütte or Poldina Hut' (Poldi Ironworks) at Komotau (now Kladno, Czech Republic). Of the 433 industrial plants involved in making parts for the Jagdpanzer 38, 316 or 76 percent of these factories were located in the Protektorat Böhmen und Mähren (Protectorate of Bohemia and Moravia) as the Czech part of the former Czechoslovakia was called after its occupation by the Third Reich. (Vladimir Francev)

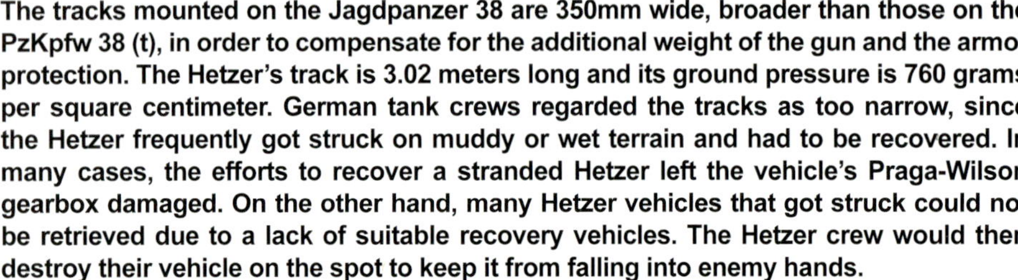

The tracks mounted on the Jagdpanzer 38 are 350mm wide, broader than those on the PzKpfw 38 (t), in order to compensate for the additional weight of the gun and the armor protection. The Hetzer's track is 3.02 meters long and its ground pressure is 760 grams per square centimeter. German tank crews regarded the tracks as too narrow, since the Hetzer frequently got struck on muddy or wet terrain and had to be recovered. In many cases, the efforts to recover a stranded Hetzer left the vehicle's Praga-Wilson gearbox damaged. On the other hand, many Hetzer vehicles that got struck could not be retrieved due to a lack of suitable recovery vehicles. The Hetzer crew would then destroy their vehicle on the spot to keep it from falling into enemy hands.

A total of 96 type Kgs 350/140 track links are mounted on the track of the Jagdpanzer 38. The track links and their headless track pins were made of manganese-nickel steel. The track shoes were connected by pins held in place by spring clips that allowed rapid changing.

The 20 teeth in the front drive sprocket engage slots in the track links in order to propel the track.

Eight bolts attach a circular cover plate onto the front drive sprocket. The cover plate is removable for maintenance or replacement of the entire sprocket. Located in the center is a nipple for lubricating the bearings with grease. The circular cover plate of the Jagdpanzer 38 is nearly identical to that of the PzKpfw 38(t).

The arch-shaped aperture in the inner front drive is adapted from the PzKpfw 38(t), the vehicle from which the Hetzer's automotive components were adopted.

The front drive sprocket of a Jagdpanzer 38 has 20 teeth – one more than on the PzKpfw 38(t) from which the Hetzer evolved. These teeth transported the manganese-nickel steel track with headless track pins. A dedicated feature of the front drive sprocket of a Jagdpanzer 38 is the lack of any circular apertures in the outer sprocket. The front drive sprockets on the PzKpfw 38(t) and the first thee production Hetzer vehicles had eight apertures. To save time in the production process, these apertures were permanently deleted, starting with the fourth production Hetzer.

The road wheels of the Jagdpanzer 38 are mounted on the semi-elliptical leaf springs. Short cranks were used to mount the wheels in pairs. The semi-elliptical leaf springs served each pair of wheels and were fixed to the hull on a single central mount.

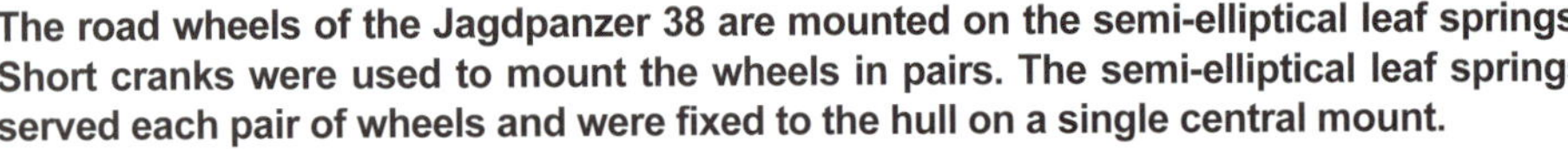

The arch-shaped aperture in the lower portion of the cap is a feature of early Hetzer vehicles. (Dénes Bernad)

On most Jagdpanzer 38 vehicles, a solid cover with a vertical rib wraps around the semi-elliptical leaf springs.

A reinforcing cap wraps surround the semi-elliptical leaf springs of a Hetzer. The forward springs consist of 16 leaves of 9mm thickness, while the rear suspension (photo) had the same number of 7mm leaves. The vertical stabilization rib was introduced on the production line of the Hetzer during September 1944. Early models of the Jagdpanzer 38 lacked this vertical stabilization rib.

Track links have two guide horns to ensure tracks remained centered on road wheels.

In contrast to the PzKpfw 38(t), which had a total of two return rollers per side, the Jagdpanzer 38 is equipped with a single return roller. These return rollers are attached by five bolts on the hull of the Hetzer. On late-production models the return roller was riveted to the hull of the Jagdpanzer 38. The return roller prevented the road wheels from being touched by the upper track.

The return rollers of the Jagdpanzer 38 all had "rubber" tires made from Buna, a synthetic rubber produced from brown coal. The return roller had a diameter of 220mm.

The Jagdpanzer 38 on exhibit at Thun has no return roller. The circular support on which a return roller would be mounted has instead been welded shut. At the factory, a circular cover plate was welded on the end of the redundant roller base, due to the fact that no return rollers were available at the time this particular Hetzer was assembled.

This is an early type of road wheel with 32 bolts on a narrow chord rim. The early road wheels were nearly identical to those of the PzKpfw 38(t), except that the Hetzer's road wheel had a diameter of 82.5cm, while the diameter of the road wheels of the PzKpfw 38(t) was a slightly smaller 77.5cm. Road wheels with 32 bolts were mounted on the Jagdpanzer 38 until August 1944.

As a non-standard feature, this particular early road wheel on the Hetzer on exhibit at Thun is riveted. Riveted road wheels, which were not available before October 1944, were introduced because the bolts holding the rim on the road wheel tended to work themselves loose. Riveted road wheels had a life span of about 300 kilometers. It is assumed that the rivets replaced the original bolts on this particular road wheel.

The first road wheels with 16 instead of 32 bolts became available in September 1944. This wheel still has the narrow chord rim that became typical for early-production road wheels. A non-standard feature is that these wheels were riveted, rather than bolted.

The circular center panel of the Jagdpanzer 38 was fixed to the wheel with 16 bolts. This covering could be removed for maintenance purposes. A nipple in the center of the road wheel was used to lubricate the bearings with grease. This circular panel was taken over directly from the PzKpfw 38(t). One bolt is missing on this circular covering. Missing bolts became most common during the operation of the Jagdpanzer 38 Hetzer. The circular covering mounted in the center of the road wheel remained unchanged during the production cycle of the Hetzer.

The wide chord rim is a typical feature of late-production road wheels. This particular wheel, however, on the Hetzer displayed at Thun, Switzerland, has the 32 bolts that are a feature of early-production road wheels.

The two rear left road wheels of the Hetzer on exhibit at Thun, Switzerland, are of different designs. The brown road wheel has a narrow chord and is riveted, while the green road wheel on the rear has a wide chord rim that is held in place by 32 rivets. The rubber rings were made of Buna, a type of synthetic rubber.

Thirty-two bolts hold the wide chord rim of this Hetzer road wheel in place. This road wheel, with its vulcanized rubber ring, is mounted on the Jagdpanzer 38 Hetzer on exhibit at the Armor Museum at Thun, Switzerland.

The welded bases of the road wheel joints are fixed to the bottom of the hull with screws. There were two bases for two joints each on each side of the hull.

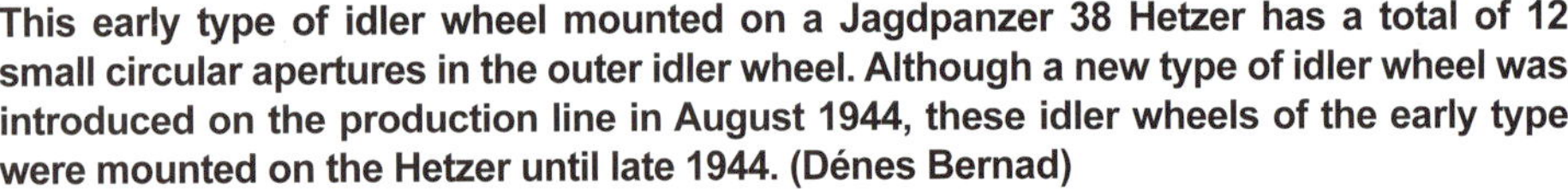

This early type of idler wheel mounted on a Jagdpanzer 38 Hetzer has a total of 12 small circular apertures in the outer idler wheel. Although a new type of idler wheel was introduced on the production line in August 1944, these idler wheels of the early type were mounted on the Hetzer until late 1944. (Dénes Bernad)

Simplified idler wheels with eight apertures were introduced on the Jagdpanzer 38 for the first time during August 1944 but were rarely used on that vehicle. The idlers have a diameter of 53.5cm – slightly larger than the 53.3cm idler mounted on the PzKpfw 38(t).

In order to speed up production, an idler wheel with six apertures in the disc was introduced on the production line at BMM and Škoda during November 1944. BMM at Praha-Libeň continued to equip the Hetzer with this type of idler wheel until the end of the war, while Škoda phased out the six-aperture idler wheel in March 1945.

The idler wheel with four large apertures is a very distinctive feature of Jagdpanzer 38 Hetzer vehicles built by Škoda at Pilsen. This idler was introduced for the first time on the production line during April 1945. Hetzer vehicles built by the Böhmisch-Mährische Maschinenfabriken AG (Bohemian-Moravian Machines Factory Limited or "BMM") at Praha-Libeň were never equipped with this type of idler wheel.

The circular access panel on the idler wheel of this Jagdpanzer 38 is held in place with nine bolts. The panel can be removed for inspection purposes.

The idler wheel of a Jagdpanzer 38 is photographed from below. Like the outer disc, the inner disc of this particular Hetzer on exhibit at Thun has eight circular apertures. A dedicated feature for the Hetzer is the additional armor plate located under the swing arm. The PzKpfw 38(t) had no such plate.

The swing arm for the right idler wheel is connected to the track tension adjuster located on the rear armor plate of the Jagdpanzer 38. The track tension adjuster was able to move the swing arm 165mm forward or backward in order to obtain the necessary tension for the track.

Additional armor is welded on the lower armor plate of the Jagdpanzer 38, just around the right idler wheel. The lower protection plate of the hull has a thickness of 8mm.

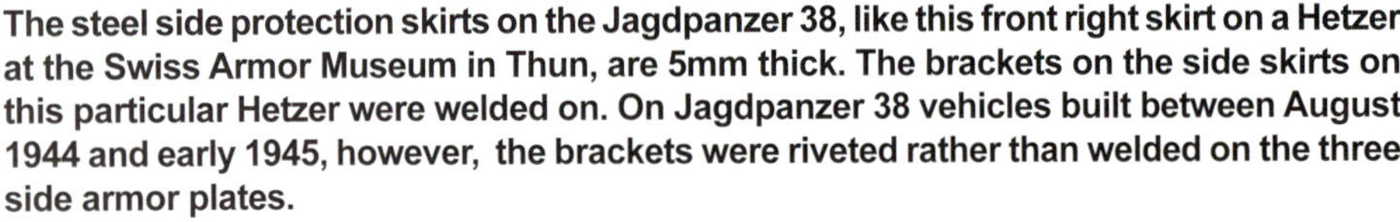

The steel side protection skirts on the Jagdpanzer 38, like this front right skirt on a Hetzer at the Swiss Armor Museum in Thun, are 5mm thick. The brackets on the side skirts on this particular Hetzer were welded on. On Jagdpanzer 38 vehicles built between August 1944 and early 1945, however, the brackets were riveted rather than welded on the three side armor plates.

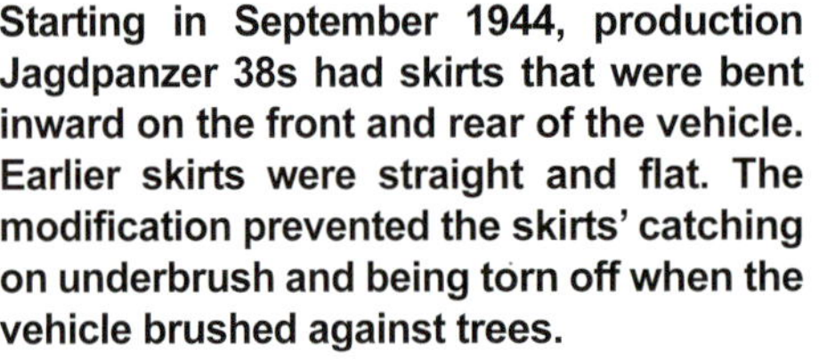

Starting in September 1944, production Jagdpanzer 38s had skirts that were bent inward on the front and rear of the vehicle. Earlier skirts were straight and flat. The modification prevented the skirts' catching on underbrush and being torn off when the vehicle brushed against trees.

The bracket of the Jagdpanzer 38 Hetzer was welded to the inner surface of the protection skirts. A bolt welded on the armor plate held the bracket in place on the superstructure. This configuration remained virtually unchanged during the production cycle of the Jagdpanzer 38.

The end of the rear right protection skirt on this Jagdpanzer 38 bends inward. Bent skirt ends were introduced on the production line during September 1944 and remained until the end of the production cycle of the Hetzer. The front and rear end of the protective skirts were bent inward to prevent their being torn off by underbrush.

This right rear bracket connects the side protection skirts with the rear superstructure of a Jagdpanzer 38 Hetzer. The rear-bracket design was different from that of the other side brackets connecting the skirts with the superstructure of the Jagdpanzer 38.

Jagdpanzer 38 Hetzer
Early Variant (June 1944)

Length:	6.27m (4.87m without barrel)
Width:	2.65m
Height:	2.10m
Weight (loaded):	16 tons
Powerplant:	Praga AC 2800 petrol engine with an output of 160HP Displacement 7754 cubiccm.
Transmission:	Praga Wilson Model 6 gearbox (five forward / one reverse)
Speed:	40 km/h (road), 25 km/h (off road)
Range:	180 km (road), 130 km (off road)
Armament:	1 Rheinmetall - Borsig Pak 39 L/48 7.5cm gun with an ammunition supply of 40 rounds. 1 MG 34 7.92mm with an ammunition supply of 600 rounds.
Crew:	4

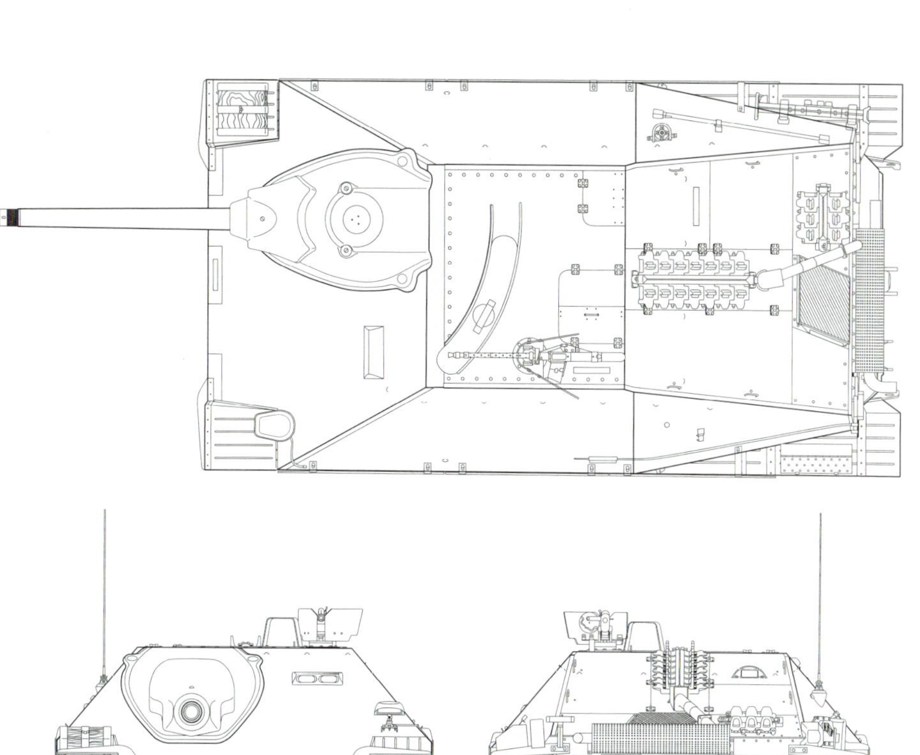

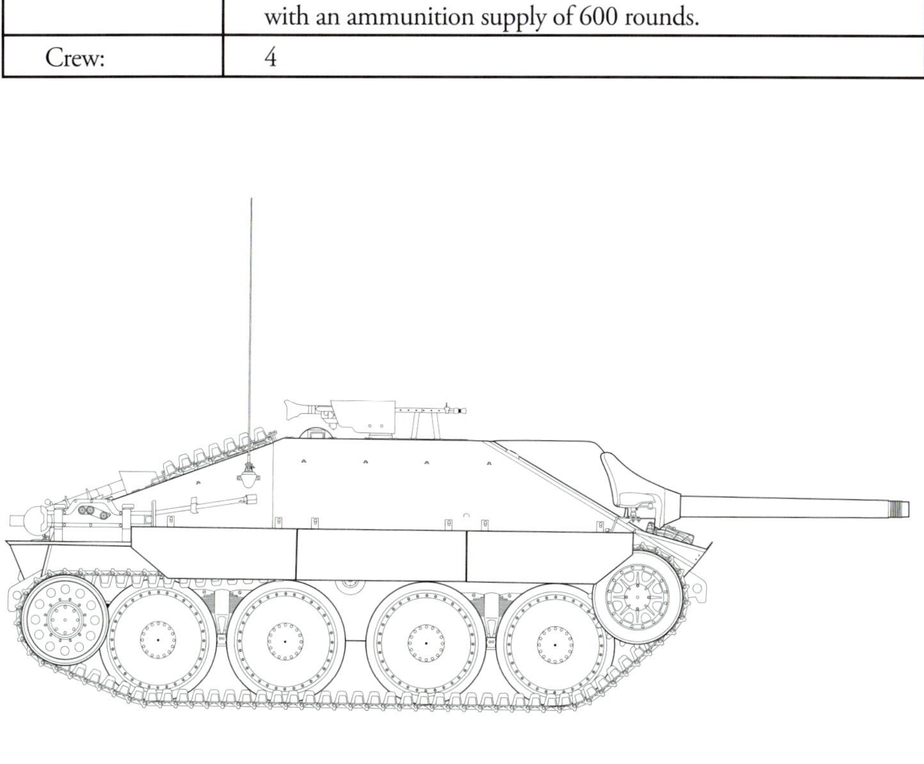

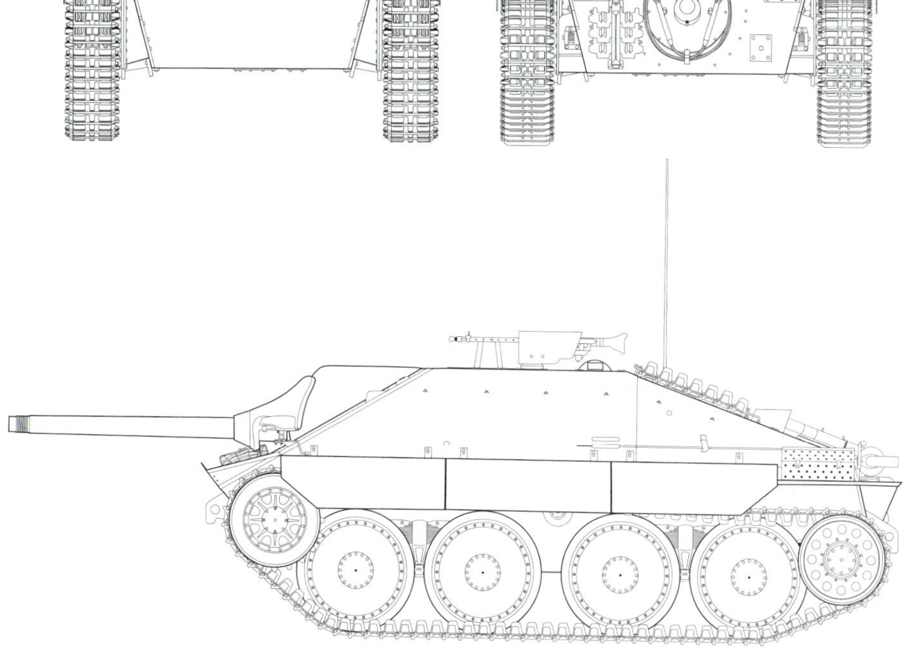

An 8mm-thick armor plate screwed on the superstructure of the Jagdpanzer 38 protects the vehicle's crew compartment. At the front is the banana-shaped sliding plate that covers the hatch for the gunner's Sfl ZF1a gunsight. This early Hetzer lacks the three sockets welded on medium- and late-production variants of the Jagdpanzer 38. The circular platform on the left is the mount for the flexible machine gun stand. Just behind the socket is the gunner's two-piece hatch. The gunner opened the hatch to reload the ammunition drums of the remotely operated 7.92mm MG 34 machine gun. (Dénes Bernad)

A rear-opening hatch for the commander was been introduced on the right upper crew compartment in September 1944. Early variants of the Hetzer had smaller hatches but without the rear door. (Walter Hodel)

This periscope, intended for the gunner, is mounted on top of the left side of the roof of a Jagdpanzer 38. A steel hoop protects the periscope from damage. No periscope could be mounted on the right side of the roof because of the presence of the right-offset mounting of the Pak 39 L/48 gun. As a result, the crew was blind on the right side.

A steel hoop protects the Sfl ZF1a gunsight that was operated by the gunner. Its angle of view was eight degrees with a three times magnification. At the rear is the armor shield for the MG 34.

A circular aperture for the commander's periscope is cut in the banana-shaped sliding armor plate of this particular Hetzer on exhibit at the Armor Museum at Thun. A protection hoop for the absent periscope is welded on the sliding plate. Located just on the upper left edge of the sliding plate is one of a total of three sockets into which a folding jib-crane could be installed on the roof of the Hetzer. (Walter Hodel)

The V-shaped armor shield for the MG 34 machine gun as shown from the rear. Hetzer crews disliked the remote operated MG 34 because of its poor accuracy. Some crews mounted a 7.92mm MG 42 machine gun on the rear engine decking of the Jagdpanzer 38 as a field modification.

A V-shaped armor shield protects the front of the mount for the MG 34 machine gun, which the gunner, inside the crew compartment, operated by remote control. The mount allowed a 360° field of fire, but elevation was limited to +12° and depression to -6°. The ammunition supply for the MG 34 was 600 rounds, divided into 12 drums.

The Swiss Army's Armor Museum at Thun exhibits this Jagdpanzer 38 with its collection of foreign tank models. This abandoned former Wehrmacht Hetzer was collected by a Swiss salvage team operating in the French occupation zone of Germany in May 1949.

The Jagdpanzer 38 on exhibit in the Armor Museum at Thun is painted with a fictional camouflage and has a fictional tactical number applied. The identity and the manufacturer number of this Hetzer are still unknown. Many parts of its equipment are missing, such as the Notek blackout light and several tools that were stored on the superstructure of the vehicle. Also part of the museum's collection of foreign armored vehicles are two additional German tank destroyers, the Jagdpanzer IV, as well the Jagdpanther Ausf G1, which are on exhibit in the background.

For some unknown reason, both rear fenders above the idler wheel on this Jagdpanzer 38 Hetzer are bent. Such bent fenders were never used in operation by the German Wehrmacht during World War II. This Jagdpanzer 38 is on exhibit next to a PzKpfw IV Ausf J, which a Swiss Army salvage team also retrieved from France after the end of World War II. This Hetzer had an astonishing mix of road wheels of different types when it was shipped to Switzerland aboard a flatcar in 1949. The Armor Museum of the Swiss Army is located in the vast proving ground of the Swiss Army at Thun. A Leopard main battle tank of the Swiss Army drives past in the background.

The entire hull for the Jagdpanzer 38 Hetzer was manufactured by the Komotauer Edelstahlhütte AG, the former Poldihütte or Poldina Hut' (Poldi Ironworks) at Komotau (now Kladno, Czech Republic). The Komotauer Edelstahlhütte AG became the sole manufacturer for the hull for the Hetzer in World War II. The hull was shiped on railway flat cars to the two assembling plants, the Böhmisch-Mährische Maschinenfabriken AG (Bohemian-Moravian Machines Factory Limited) at Praha-Libeň or the Skodawerke (Škoda works) at Pilsen (now Plzeň, Czech Republic). (Vladimir Francev)

Skilled and unsklled workers of the Böhmisch-Mährische Maschinenfabriken AG fit out the hulls of the Jagpanzer 38. These hulls were all delivered from the Komotauer Edelstahlhütte AG at Komotau. The chassis as well the automotive components were all taken over from the well-proven PzKpfw 38(t) tank, which BMM built between May 1939 and June 1942. The unit price of a single Hetzer was quoted with 54,000 Reichsmark. (Vladimir Francev)

This particular Jagdpanzer 38 arrived at the Swiss Army's proving ground of Thun in the Berner Oberland on a French railway flat car on 10 September 1945. This particular Jagdpanzer 38 was captured by the French Army on the Western front. This Jagdpanzer 38 was in ready to run condition, but lacked the German Notek blackout light usually mounted at the left fender. The entire vehicle was painted in olive green by the French Army before it was handed over to the Swiss Army. (Swiss Federal Archives)

Due to the restricted space available in the crew compartment, the Rheinmetall-Borsig Pak 39 L/48 gun was offset to the right. Only the left side and the rear of the recoil guard have a solid protection. A pad made of Buna – a synthetic rubber made of brown coal – was mounted inside the rear solid recoil guard. The cardan drive shaft has been protected with a tube shaped covering and passes through the entire crew compartment. The Praga AC 2800 engine had a displacement of 7,754 cubic centimeters. (Swiss Federal Archives)

Pak 39 L/48 Gun

The formidable Rheinmetall-Borsig Pak 39 L/48 7.5cm anti tank gun was the tank variant of the widely used Pak 40 anti tank gun. Production of the dedicated Pak 39 L/48 tank destroyer weapon started in 1943 and it became the standard anti tank weapon of the Wehrmacht during World War II. A total of 6,000 Pak 39 L/48 were built by the Rheinmetall-Borsig AG at Unterlüss and the Seitz-Werke GmbH at Bad Kreuznach. The gun saw service with the Jagdpanzer 38 Hetzer and the Jagdpanzer IV L/48 tank destroyers. The Pak 39 L/48 had a muzzle velocity of 750 meters per second and a barrel life of 5,000 to 7,000 rounds. German crews praised the Pak 39 L/48 in the Hetzer as a very accurate weapon that penetrated the armor of a Soviet T-34 main battle tank at distances up to 800 meters.

The Pak 39 was originally intended to be mounted in the center of a vehicle, so all controls and safety switches were located on the interior right side of the Jagdpanzer 38 Hetzer, where the loader should have been positioned. But because the Hetzer's hull was narrow, the 7.5cm gun was mounted as close to the right side of the vehicle as possible, forcing the loader to feed the gun from the wrong side, reach across the gun to switch off the safety, and reach under or across the recoil path of the gun to retrieve most of the stowed ammunition. The charging lever was attached on the right rear of the breech.

The 7.5cm gun was installed on a cardan joint in the glacis and a cast ball mount was fixed to the upper side of the glacis. The gun cradle with a hydraulic brake and pneumatic counter recoil mechanism reduced the recoil to 630mm.

The upper interior of the crew compartment in a standard production Jagdpanzer 38 Hetzer was painted in Elfenbein RAL 1001 (ivory), while lower areas and floors were left in Rotbraun RAL 8012 (red primer).

The upper hand wheel of the Rheinmetall-Borsig Pak 39 L/48 sets the gun's elevation. The horizontal traverse is set by the hand wheel located below. The motion of the wheel for the horizontal traverse was provided via a cardan shaft as well a gearbox with a worm gear. (Swiss Federal Archives)

Only the left side of the recoil guard had solid protection. (Swiss Federal Archives)

The small hand wheel mounded on the left, just above the upper hand wheel, is for the fine tuning of the elevation. This wheel was deleted on the Pak 40 gun in the Swiss G 13 tank destroyers. Located below the breech is the ribbed casing of the Praga-Wilson gearbox. (Swiss Federal Archives)

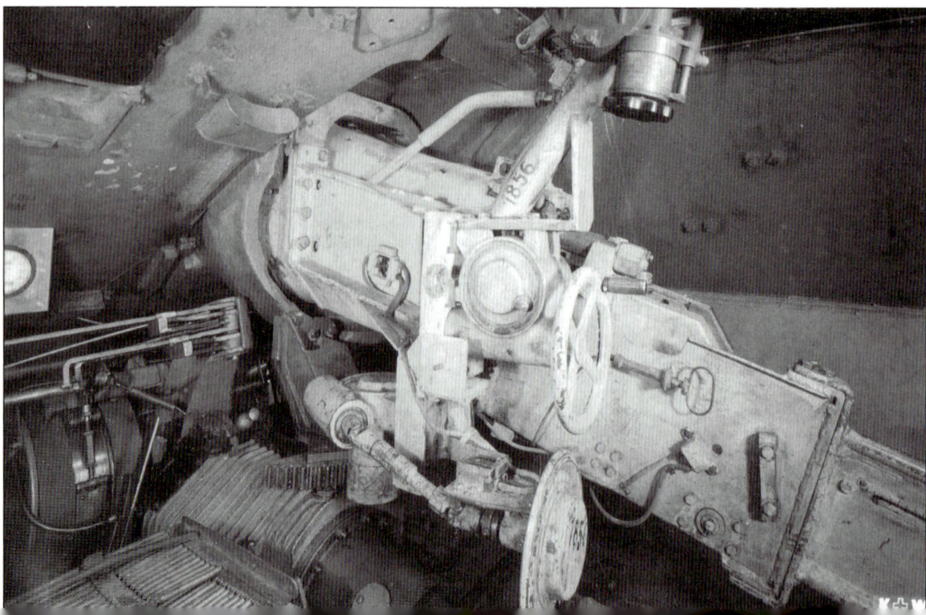

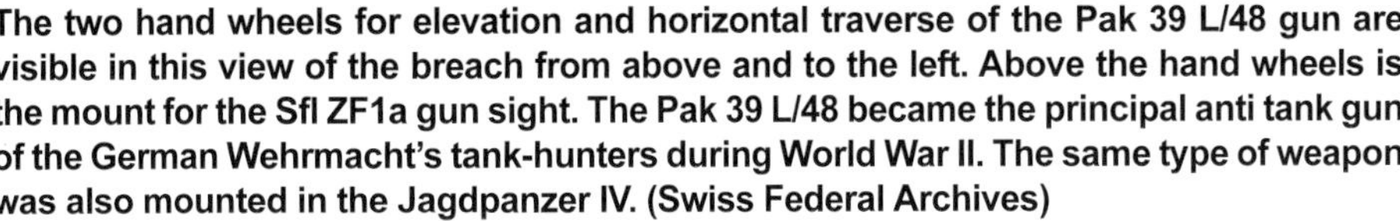

The two hand wheels for elevation and horizontal traverse of the Pak 39 L/48 gun are visible in this view of the breach from above and to the left. Above the hand wheels is the mount for the Sfl ZF1a gun sight. The Pak 39 L/48 became the principal anti tank gun of the German Wehrmacht's tank-hunters during World War II. The same type of weapon was also mounted in the Jagdpanzer IV. (Swiss Federal Archives)

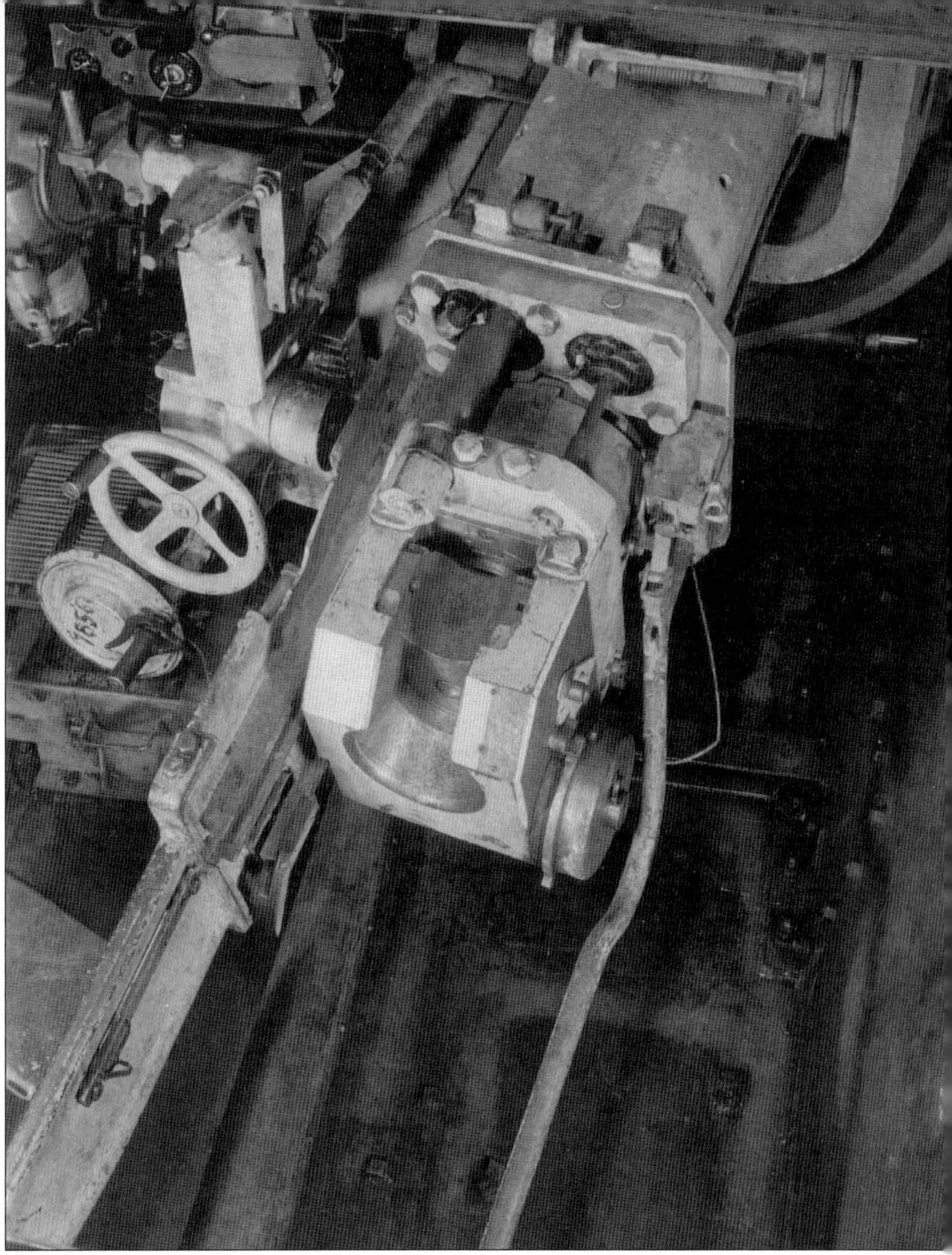

The breech of the Rheinmetall-Borsig Pak 39 L/48 7.5cm gun is viewed from the top right. Four pairs of wedges fitted between the mantlet and the glacis transmitted the recoil from the Pak 39 L/48 to the vehicle. This arrangement allowed designers to dispense with a muzzle brake on the gun. The Pak 39 L/48 weighed 428 kilograms. (Swiss Federal Archives)

This Jagdpanzer 38 was built by Škoda at Pilsen (now Plzeň, Czech Republic) and underwent factory test trials before being turned over to the Wehrmacht. This Hetzer has the early horizontal muffler configuration that was built until September 1944. A vertical mounted exhaust pipe with an integrated flame damper was introduced in October 1944 and the horizontal muffler deleted. The engine compartment of the Jagdpanzer 38 was protected by 8mm armor plates, which were mounted at an angle of 70 degrees. Like the roof armor plate, the armor plate for the engine compartment was screwed down to the superstructure. The Praga AC 2800 engine was accessed through two access doors, which were staggered. The rhomboid-shaped air exhaust is covered with a mesh, and the airflow is regulated with a slide. On the base of the armor plate for the engine compartment are square access hatches for the fuel tanks (left) and the radiator filler (right). A spare track was located on the centerline of the armor plate protecting the engine bay. (Vladimir Francev)

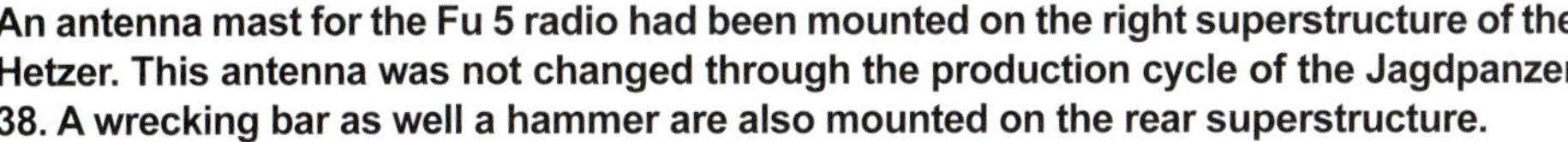

An antenna mast for the Fu 5 radio had been mounted on the right superstructure of the Hetzer. This antenna was not changed through the production cycle of the Jagdpanzer 38. A wrecking bar as well a hammer are also mounted on the rear superstructure.

The periscope located on the upper right armor plate was manned by the commander and provided the crew with rear vision. A massive steel hoop, secured by two rivets to the 8mm armor plate, protects the rear periscope from damage.

The curved metal cover for the exhaust pipe on this vehicle is a non-standard feature that was directly adopted from the PzKpfw 38(t). Only a few of the early Jagdpanzer 38 vehicles were equipped with this type of cover. The rhomboid air exhaust was also taken over from the last version of the PzKpfw 38(t) Ausf G. The air intake remained unchanged through the production cycle of the Hetzer. (Dénes Bernad)

The square exhaust pipe's metal cover of the Praga AC 2800 powerplant became standard for the Jagdpanzer 38 Hetzer in the production cycle of this German tank destroyer. Squared covers on the standard production Jagdpanzer 38 Hetzer vehicles were made from metal sheets welded together to speed up production process. The curved metal covers employed on the first production models of the Jagdpanzer 38 were all cast.

A feature for early Jagdpanzer 38s is the horizontal muffler, which was covered with a mesh heat guard. Hetzer in this horizontal muffler configuration were delivered by BMM and Škoda until September 1944.

The exhaust pipe had been slanted to the right in order not to interfere with the rhomboid shaped air exhaust, which is equipped with a slide for airflow regulation.

The bent exhaust pipe was located on the left side of the muffler. This curved pipe was a direct take over from the PzKpfw 38(t).

A mesh head guard covered the muffler on the early production models of the Jagdpanzer 38. In August 1944, the head guard was deleted from the horizontal muffler on Jagdpanzer 38s built by BMM and Škoda.

The vertical flame damper cowling surrounding the exhaust pipe was introduced on the production line of BMM and Škoda during October 1944. A shortcoming of gasoline-powered engines was that they gave off hot exhaust gases that glowed and could be easily spotted by enemy forces at night. Diesel powered tanks such as the Soviet T-34 had much lower exhaust temperatures. The Hetzer's flame damper not only took care of the glowing exhaust problem but also eliminated engine backfires. A massive disadvantage of the flame damper was the fact that it generated much more noise than the original horizontal, cylindrical muffler. The vertical muffler avoided trapping grenades, which might land on the engine deck. On most Jagdpanzer 38s the flame damper was slanted to the right. The very last Hetzer built by Škoda during April 1945 had a straight flame damper, however. BMM used the slanted flame damper configuration until the end of production. (Walter Hodel)

The tubular flame damper is attached with a profile to the lower rear armor plate of the engine compartment. On some Jagdpanzer 38s, the flame damper was fixed with a profile to the upper rear armor plate. On this particular Hetzer, profile is fixed on the engine compartment.

The exhaust pipe has been embedded in the tubular flame damper. This design hid the glowing exhaust and eliminated backfires.

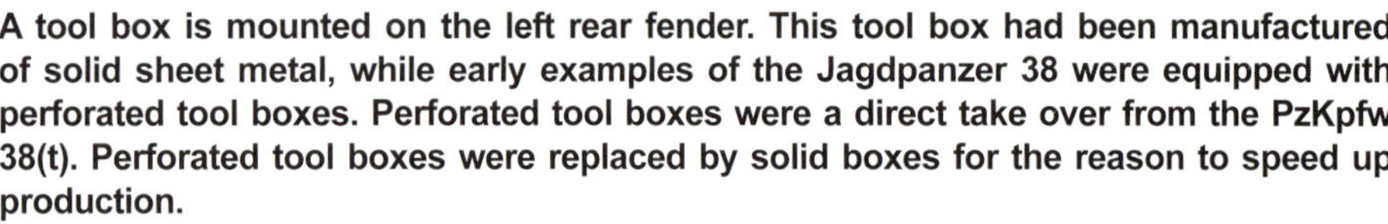

A tool box is mounted on the left rear fender. This tool box had been manufactured of solid sheet metal, while early examples of the Jagdpanzer 38 were equipped with perforated tool boxes. Perforated tool boxes were a direct take over from the PzKpfw 38(t). Perforated tool boxes were replaced by solid boxes for the reason to speed up production.

The covering for the tool box was held in place with a leather pin. The tool box contained among other items two S-shaped hooks.

The jack was located on the right rear fender. The jack was held in place by a snap fastener on the fender. The right rear superstructure of the Jagdpanzer 38 hold a wrecking bar and a hammer.

The port rear fender has a snap fastener to accommodate the jack. The fastener on the rear superstructure housed the wreckling bar. This wreckling-bar configuration remained unchanged through the Jagdpanzer 38 Hetzer production cycle. The wreckling bar is not mounted on this particular exhbit at the Armor Museum at Thun, Switzerland.

One of a total of two handles that were welded on the left armor door protecting the engine bay of a Jagdpanzer 38.

Apart from late production Jagdpanzer 38s built by Škoda in April 1945, all other Hetzers had two hinges on the right access hatch. Almost all Hetzer had a centerline mounted handle welded on the lower part of the hatch. This Jagdpanzer 38 on exhibit at Thun has one of the two hinges missing. This hatch for the radiator filler was cut in the lower right armor plate of the rear engine bay for the first time during July 1944 at the production line of the Jagdpanzer 38. This modification prevented the Hetzer crews to open the heavy armor plate when adding cooling water for the radiator of the Praga AC 2800 engine with an output of 160 hp. The access hatch was cut in the rear armor plate after receiving complaints from the Hetzer crews serving on the Western and Eastern front.

The provision to carry a shovel on the rear right superstructure is a dedicated feature for very late Jagdpanzer 38 built in April 1945 by Škoda at Pilsen (now Plzeň). All Hetzer built by BMM lacked this provision to carry a shovel on the right superstructure. The shovel was secured by a band of sheet metal welded on the superstructure.

Late production Jagdpanzer 38 built by Škoda had a single hinge riveted on the right access panel. Most of all Hetzer had two hinges instead. The single hinge configuration was never introduced on Jagdpanzer 38 built by BMM. The last Hetzer manufactured by Škoda in April 1945 had a vertical handle welded on the right side of the hatch. BMM never adopted this vertical handle configuration and remained on the horizontal handle configuration. This late type of access hatch was subsequently adopted by the G 13 for Switzerland.

Jagdpanzer built until September 1944

Horizontal mounted cylindrical muffler

Heat guard deleted from the muffler in August 1944

Flame Damper Development

Jagdpanzer 38 built in October 1944

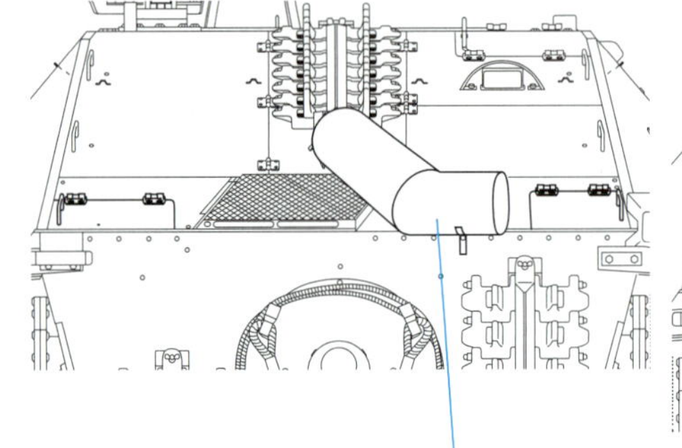

Vertical mounted exhaust pipe with integrated flame damper

Jagdpanzer 38 built by Škoda in April 1945

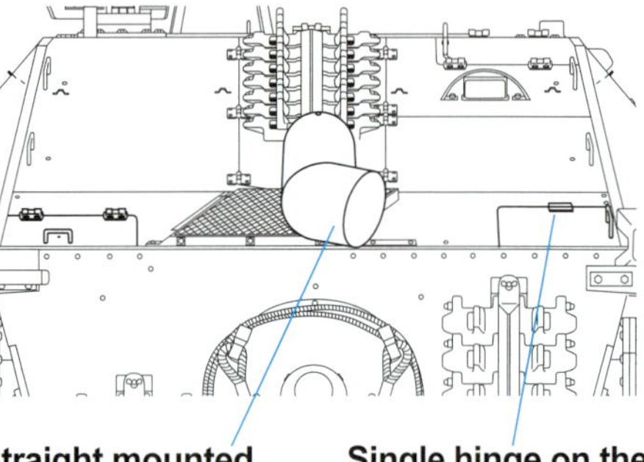

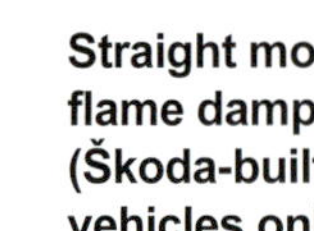

Straight mounted flame damper (Škoda-built vehicles only)

Single hinge on the right hatch on Škoda-built late-production Jagdpanzer 38

The fuel filler hatch, located on the left rear armor plate, was introduced in December 1944. Prior to the introduction of this hatch, crews had to open the large and heavy door covering the engine compartment in order to refuel the Jagdpanzer 38. The handle was vertically welded on the fuel filler hatch of all Hetzer throughout its production cycle.

The left filler hatch, here seen open, was closed with the help of a key. This filler hatch belongs to a Swiss G 13, but late production Jagdpanzer 38 vehicles were equipped with an identical hatch. The fuel filler hatches had two hinges throughout the production cycle.

Jagdpanzer 38 Hetzer Late Variant

Length:	6.27m (4.87m without barrel)
Width:	2.65m
Height:	2.10m
Weight (loaded):	16 tons
Powerplant:	Praga AC 2800 petrol engine with an output of 160HP Displacement 7754 cubic centimeters.
Transmission:	Praga Wilson Model 6 gearbox (five forward / one reverse)
Speed:	40km/h (road), 25km/h (off road)
Range:	180km (road), 130km (off road)
Armament:	1 Rheinmetall - Borsig Pak 39 L/48 7.5cm gun with an ammunition supply of 45 rounds. 1 MG 34 7.92mm with an ammunition supply of 600 rounds.
Crew:	4

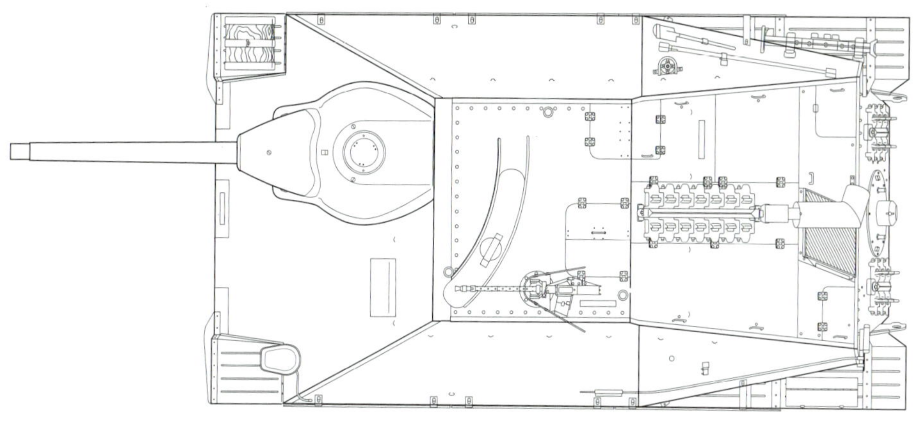

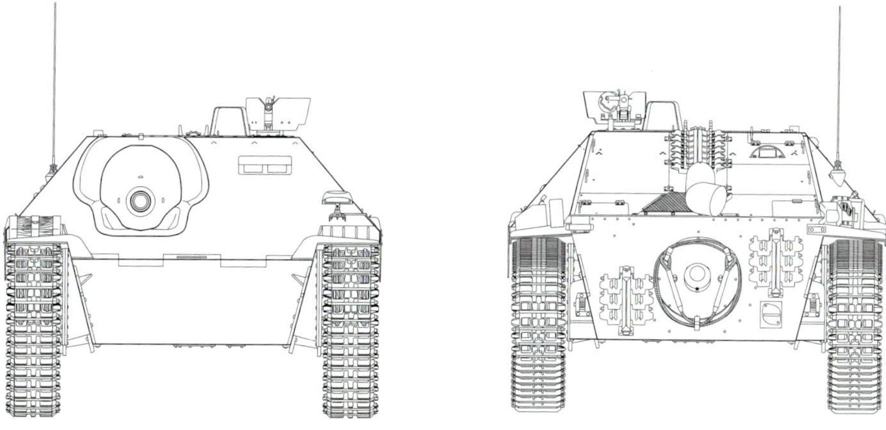

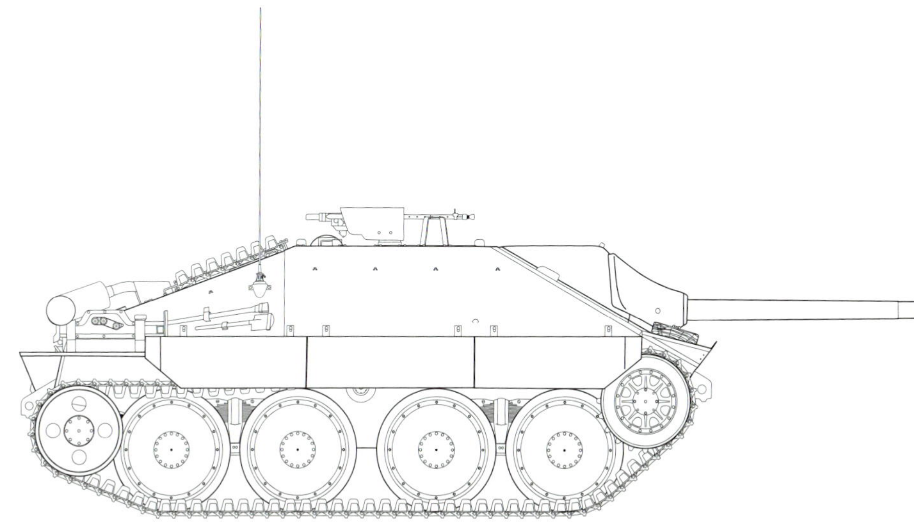

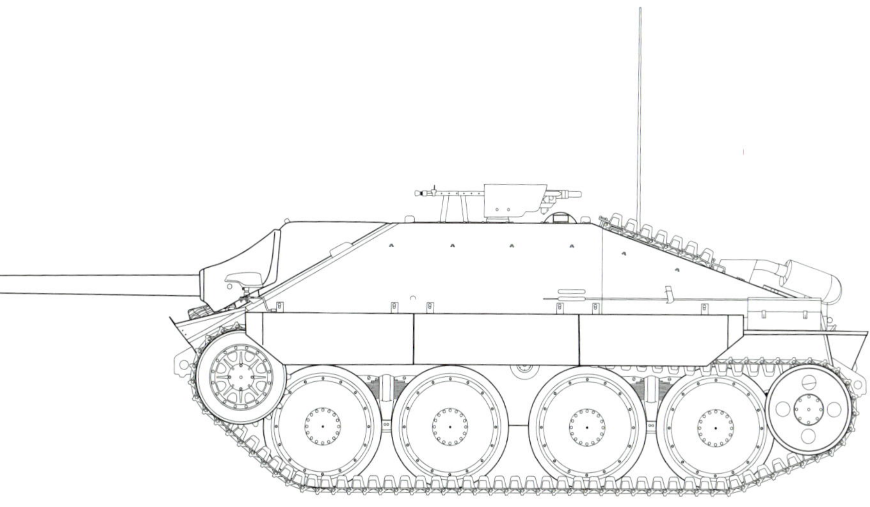

The circular cover plate of the fan was a direct take over from the PzKpfw 38(t). The cover plate for the shaft of the hand crank is missing from this Hetzer on exhibit at Thun. The rear armor plate is 8mm thick and slopes at 15 degrees.

The tow cable has been stored on the circular armor plate. A total of three hooks were welded on the circular cover plate of the fan to facilitate securing the tow cable properly. These hooks were a dedicated feature for the Jagdpanzer 38, since no such hooks were ever welded on the PzKpfw 38(t).

The conical covering for the external start crank was a direct take over from the PzKpfw 38(t) Ausf G. This conical covering remained unchanged through the production cycle of the Jagdpanzer 38. The cover was attached with a snap-fit system on the circular rear armored access panel of the fan.

Notek Convoy Light

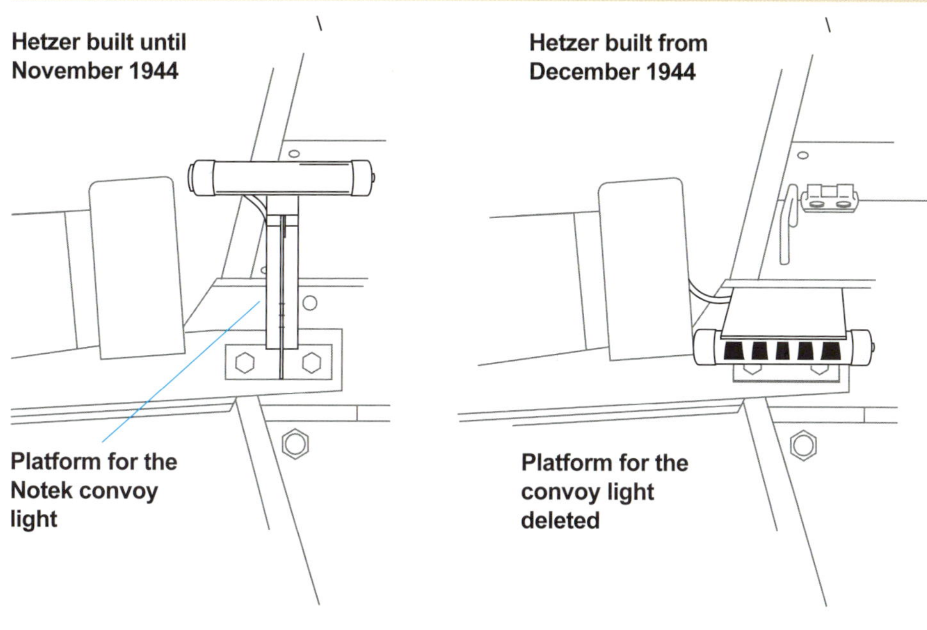

A feature of early-production Jagdpanzer 38s is the covering without a step on lower right rear armor plate. No step was welded on Hetzer vehicles that left the production line before late July 1944. (Dénes Bernad)

A step was welded on a square shaped block on Jagdpanzer 38s built in the beginning of August 1944. Hetzers built before August 1944 lacked this step. This step became available on the right side of the rear armor plate only. No step was ever provided on the left side.

The step on the lower right rear armor plate had a triangle shaped support hat was welded vertically.

The early-production Jagdpanzer 38 vehicles were equipped with a heat guard wrapped around the muffler. A number of early-production Hetzer vehicles were equipped with a towing hook attached on top of the rear armor plate. (Vladimir Francev)

In August 1944, the perforated heat guard around the muffler was deleted and Hetzer vehicles built in September 1944 were the last to be equipped with a horizontally mounted cylindrical muffler. Three additional spare track links were mounted on the right rear armor plate. The Notek convoy light was mounted on a platform attached to the left fender. A standard feature of later vehicle models was the presence of two engine-bay access hatches mounted on the base of the armor plate. This Hetzer has no such access hatches. (Vladimir Francev)

A vertical mounted exhaust pipe with an integrated flame damper was introduced in October 1944. The platform for the Notek convoy light mounted on the left bracket of the rear fender was deleted in December 1944 and the convoy light was mounted directly on the bracket for the rear fender. The hatch for the radiator filler located in the lower right armor plate of the engine bay received a horizontally welded handle in September 1944. During December 1944 an access hatch to fill the fuel tanks was cut in the lower left armor plate of the engine bay. (Vladimir Francev)

The track tension adjuster mounted on the early-production examples of the Jagdpanzer 38 were a direct take over from the PzKpfw 38(t). On late-production variants of the PzKpfw 38(t) the track tension adjuster was protected by a semicircular cover, but this cover was dropped at the start of the production of the Hetzer. Four bolts attached the rectangular track tension adjuster to the end plate. A swing arm connected to the idler wheel was used to turn the screw in either direction in order to tighten or loosen the track. Rectangular shaped track tension adjuster were mounted until October 1944 on Jagdpanzer 38 built by BMM and Škoda. This Jagdpanzer 38 is equipped with the early type of a rear towing bracket that became standard on Hetzer vehicles manufactured until October 1944. (Dénes Bernad)

The rear towing bracket of a Jagdpanzer 38 built in late 1944. This bracket, first introduced during November 1944, is shaped differently from those mounted on the early production examples of the Hetzer.

This type of tension track adjuster on the left and right rear armor plate was introduced for the first time in November 1944. Only three bolts fixed the triangular track tension adjuster with the end plate. With the introduction of the triangle shaped track tension adjuster was also the shape of the housing for the idler wheel altered.

A late wartime production Jagdpanzer 38 served as a prototype for the Swiss Panzerjäger G 13. The vehicle, rebuilt in the Škoda workshop at Plzeň (Czechoslovakia), still carries its original German ambush camouflage. The StuK 40 7.5cm assault gun has been mounted with a new armored housing for the gun ball mount and a gun mantlet. A dedicated feature for the StuK 40 gun is the muzzle brake, which was not mounted on standard Jagdpanzer 38s. The sheet-metal guard for the driver's periscope became taller on this G 13 prototype. This type of sheet metal guard was not adopted on the production G 13s for Switzerland. (Škoda Archive via Vladislav Krátký)

Swiss Panzerjäger G 13

In the spring of 1946, the Škoda factory at Plzeň offered a modified variant of the Jagdpanzer 38 to the Swiss Ministry of Defense for an unit price of 600,000 Czechoslovak Crowns (equal to 51,650 Swiss Francs). The price quoted by Škoda was only one-fifth of the vehicle's original price, making the offer appear highly favorable to the Swiss Defense Ministry. A G 13 prototype was shipped to Switzerland and tested during summer 1946 at the proving ground of the Swiss Army at Thun in the Berner Oberland region. Due to these favorable results, an order for eight pre series vehicles was placed on 4 September 1946. Škoda offered the Hetzer under the designation G 13, which was the in-house wartime production designation issued by Škoda for the Jagdpanzer 38. The Swiss subsequently adopted this designation and called the first tank destroyer in the inventory of the Swiss Army Panzerjäger G 13. The first eight G 13 vehicles were accepted by a Swiss Purchasing Delegation at Plzeň on 8 October 1946 and were shipped from the Škoda factory on 10 December 1946. Five of these G 13s (Fahrgestell-Nummer/chassis number 323 804, 323 807, 323 809, 323 823, and 323 832) were completed by Škoda as Hetzer vehicles, but could not be handled over to the German Wehrmacht because of the end of the war. These eight G 13 were still equipped with the 7.92mm MG 34 machine gun and the V-shaped armor shield, a take over from the German Jagdpanzer 38. The MG 34 and the armor shield were not mounted on the subsequent main production batches of the G 13.

The Swiss Panzerjäger G 13 was based on the latest variant of the Jagdpanzer 38 built by Škoda in April 1945. However, the G 13 featured in a number of details from the Jagdpanzer 38: The Pak 39 L/48 7.5cm gun was replaced with a Sturmkanone 40 (StuK 40) assault gun of the same caliber. In contrast to the Pak 39 L/48, which was in limited supply, there were huge quantities of the StuK 40 available in Czechoslovakia. In sharp contrast to the Jagdpanzer 38, all G 13 vehicles were equipped with a muzzle brake. Due to the slightly smaller diameter of the StuK 40, the barrel of the gun had to be increased in diameter toward the rear end, close to the gun mantlet. This enlargement became conical and allowed a proper fit of the cannon in the gun mantlet. Since the gun sight for the MG 34 machine gun was still retained on the G 13, the device was covered by an armored cupola mounted on top of the roof.

Gun Development

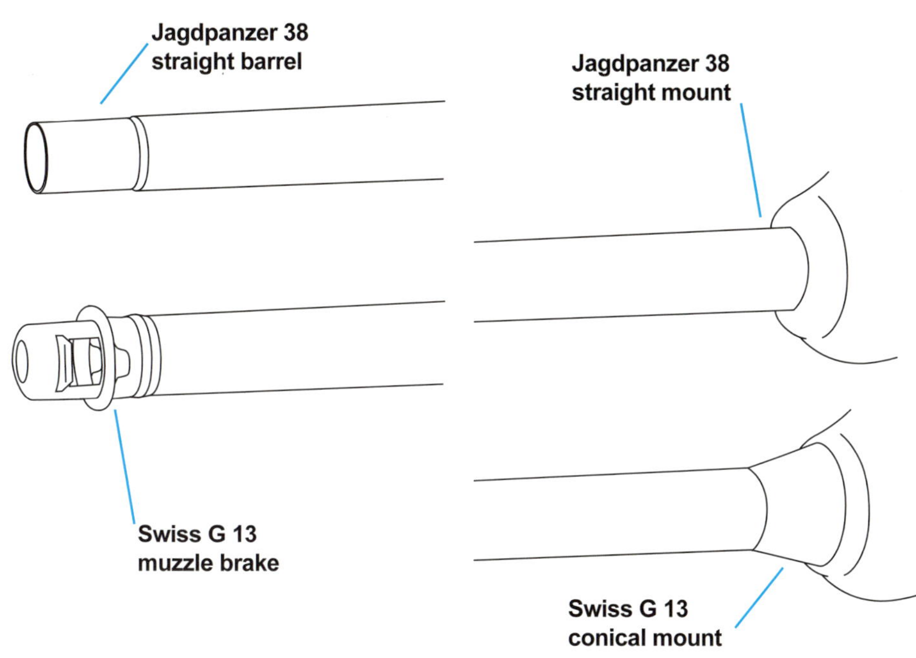

The eight pre-series G 13s were almost identical to the late production Jagdpanzer 38. The straight flame damper, the vertical handle on the access hatch on the lower engine bay armor cover plate, and the shovel mounted on the right superstructure were all a take over from very late production Jagdpanzer 38s built by Škoda in April 1945. A direct take over from the Hetzer was the Notek convoy light mounted on a platform on the left fender. Subsequent G 13s left the assembly line in Plzeň with no Notek light mounted on them. (Swiss Army via Martin Haudenschild)

Even before these eight pre-series G 13s became available for the evaluation, the Bundesrat (Swiss Federal Council) approved on 19 September 1946 an order for an additional 100 vehicles for the amount of 6 million of Swiss Francs. These G 13s were built from remaining Hetzer components that were stored at the Škoda factory at Plzeň. G 13s were delivered in the four, six and eight aperture configuration of the idler wheel as well with solid and perforated tool boxes.

A further order for 50 additional vehicles with a value of 4.7 million Swiss francs was placed by the Generalstabs Abteilung (General Staff of the Swiss Army) on 16 October 1947. These vehicles were manufactured entirely new for the Swiss Army. A total of 158 G 13s were delivered from the Škoda factory at Plzeň to the Swiss Army between 10 December 1946 and 16 February 1950. The three Panzerjäger Abteilungen 21, 22 and 23 (tank destroyer detachments 21, 22 and 23) were formed during 1949 and equipped with the G 13.

The G 13s were progressively modified by the Swiss Army. Shortly after arrival, a protection housing was welded over the right position light. In 1948 and 1949 all G 13 vehicles were retrofitted with a nipple to lubricate the final drive with oil instead of grease. The original Škoda tracks were soon worn out and replaced in 1950 with tracks manufactured in Switzerland. A housing with a drum containing 600 meters of F2-E telephone cable was mounted on the rear left armor plate in 1952. This modification enabled the crews to communicate with the infantry units by means of a telephone, which could – in contrast to the radio – not be jammed or located by the enemy. Only a few G 13 were delivered from Škoda with the original German Fu 5 radio and all vehicles were subsequently equipped with a SE-202 radio set manufactured in the United States of America. During 1952, a total of 86 G 13s were equipped with a Swiss developed Saurer CH 2DRM 8-cylinder inline Diesel engine with an output of 150 HP. The diesel engine required a major redesign of the muffler and a new air intake.

A single 7.5mm Flab Mg 38 anti aircraft machine gun was mounted centerline on the rear engine bay armor plate. The spare track links were removed from the engine bay armor plate and the exhaust lead in into the engine compartment was shortened. The muffler received a head guard. In addition, a handle was welded close to the head guard on the right armor door covering the engine compartment. The Flab Mg 38 was introduced in 1954 alongside with the spare track links and a single spare road wheel, which were mounted on the right superstructure. Three spare track links as well a square shaped ammunition box for the Flab Mg 38 was mounted on the left superstructure.

The unreliable Praga-Wilson Mintex-H gearbox was replaced by a Wilson gearbox of English origin between 1956 and 1957 on a total of 46 gas-powered G 13s. A Truppenerkennungstafel – a square aluminum plate on which unit markings were applied – was added on all G 13s in 1956. These plates were mounted on the lower front armor plate and the face of the housing for the telephone cable drum in 1956. The Swiss military phased out its last G 13s in 1973.

The nipple to lubricate the final drive was introduced on all 158 Panzerjäger G 13 vehicles of the Swiss Army between 1948 and 1949. This was a dedicated modification introduced by the Swiss Army. The nipple became necessary after the Swiss Army switched from grease to oil to lubricate the final drive of the G 13.

The license plate of this Panzerjäger G 13 (M-78039/hull number 32) had been painted on a right lower position of the upper hull, just below the lip of the gun recess. This position of the license plate became standard for the G 13. However, on the first eight pre-series G 13 vehicles, the license plate was painted centerline on an upper position of the lower front armor plate. In addition to the individual white registration number, the plate also featured the Swiss coat of arms and the red letter "M" for Militär (Army).

This red-painted nipple cover is mounted in the head of the final drive casing. The inscription "S.A.E. 80-90" stamped into the casing refers to the type of lubrication oil that was required. The cover was painted red on all 158 Swiss G 13 vehicles. (Walter Hodel)

A dedicated feature for the Swiss G 13 was the position light mounted on the right lower edge of the glacis. The German Jagdpanzer 38 was never equipped with such a position light. The Panzerjäger G 13 were delivered by Škoda at Plzeň without the armor housing and operated in this configuration during a brief period of time. The armor housing was welded in Switzerland on all 158 G 13s.

The Truppenerkennungstafel – a square aluminum plate – was fixed with four screws on the lower right front amor plate. Three-letter unit markings were applied with black temporary paint on these plates, which were introduced in 1956. At the end of the Wiederholdungskurs (repetition service) the letters had to be deleted from the plate.

A Swiss-manufactured search light was mounted just above the left fender of all 158 G 13 vehicles after their arrival in Switzerland. The platform for the light was mounted at the Škoda factory in Plzeň. This type of search light was for peacetime use only. A Notek blackout light for wartime service was stored in the engine compartment of the G 13.

The lead in of the power supply of the search light was protected by a wedge shaped armor protector. This lead in is a dedicated feature for the Swiss Panzerjäger G 13 vehicles and was not mounted on any of the German Jagdpanzer 38 Hetzer built during World War II. At the request of the Swiss army, the Škoda factory in Plzeň mounted the the armor wedge on the vehicles on its production line.

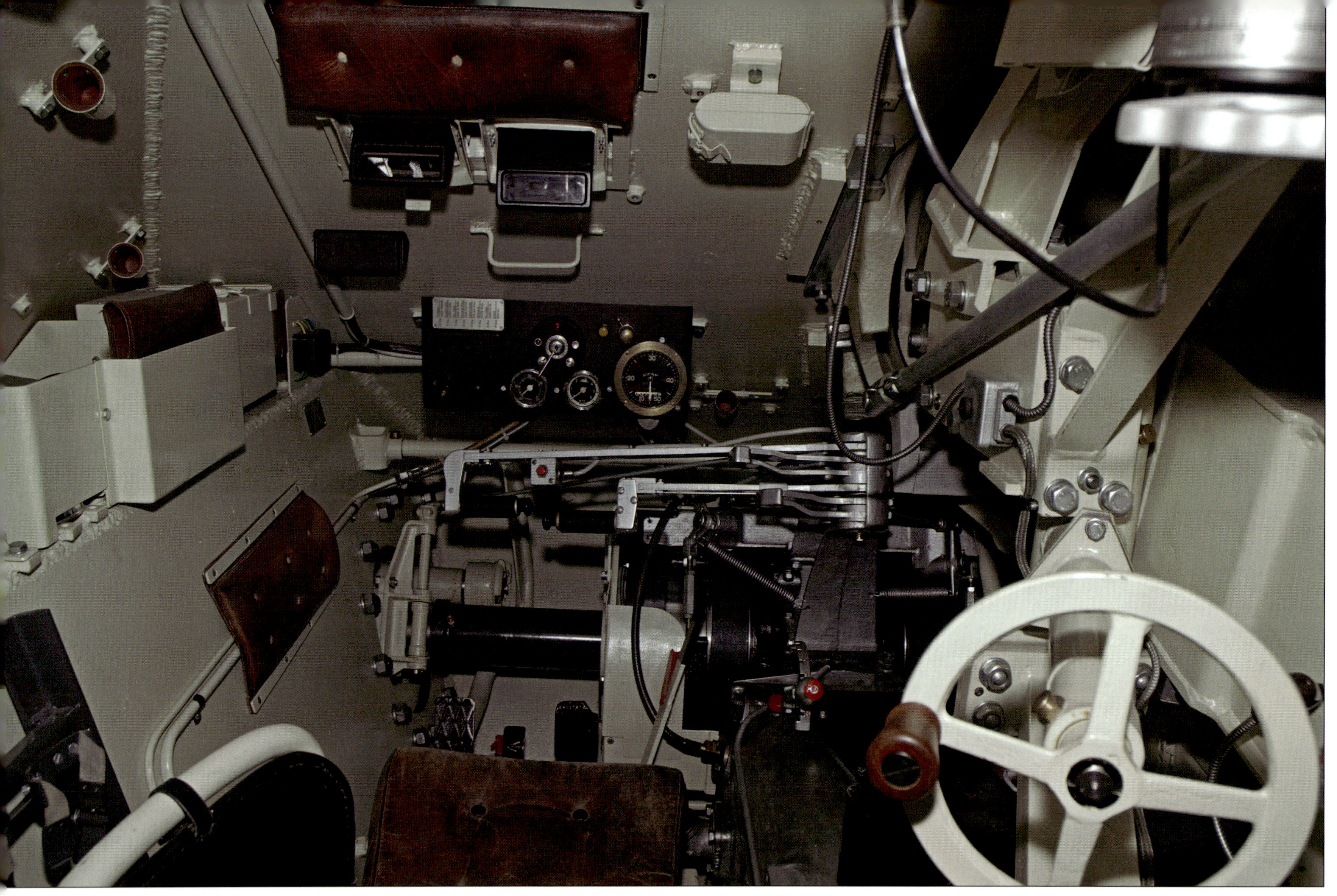

This is the crew compartment of a Swiss Panzerjäger G 13 (M-78039/hull number 32) on current exhibit in the hangar of the Collection of Historical Armor in the Swiss Army at Thun in the Berner Oberland Region. The G 13 represents the standard Swiss tank destroyer of its time. This particular G 13 was delivered to Switzerland from the Škoda factory at Plzeň on 28 July 1947. This gas powered G 13 with the original Praga AC 2800 engine (serial number 324 837) had been retrofitted with an English Wilson gearbox, replacing the original Czechoslovak Praga-Wilson Mintex-H gearbox (serial number 146), which proved to be very unreliable in service. The Swiss Panzerjäger G 13 had an ammunition supply of 40 7.5cm grenades, while late production German Jagdpanzer 38 had ammunition supply of 45 grenades. The interior of the Swiss G 13 is painted in a color close to the Elfenbein RAL 1001 (ivory) of the German Wehrmacht. The G 13 was phased out of Swiss service in 1973. (Walter Hodel)

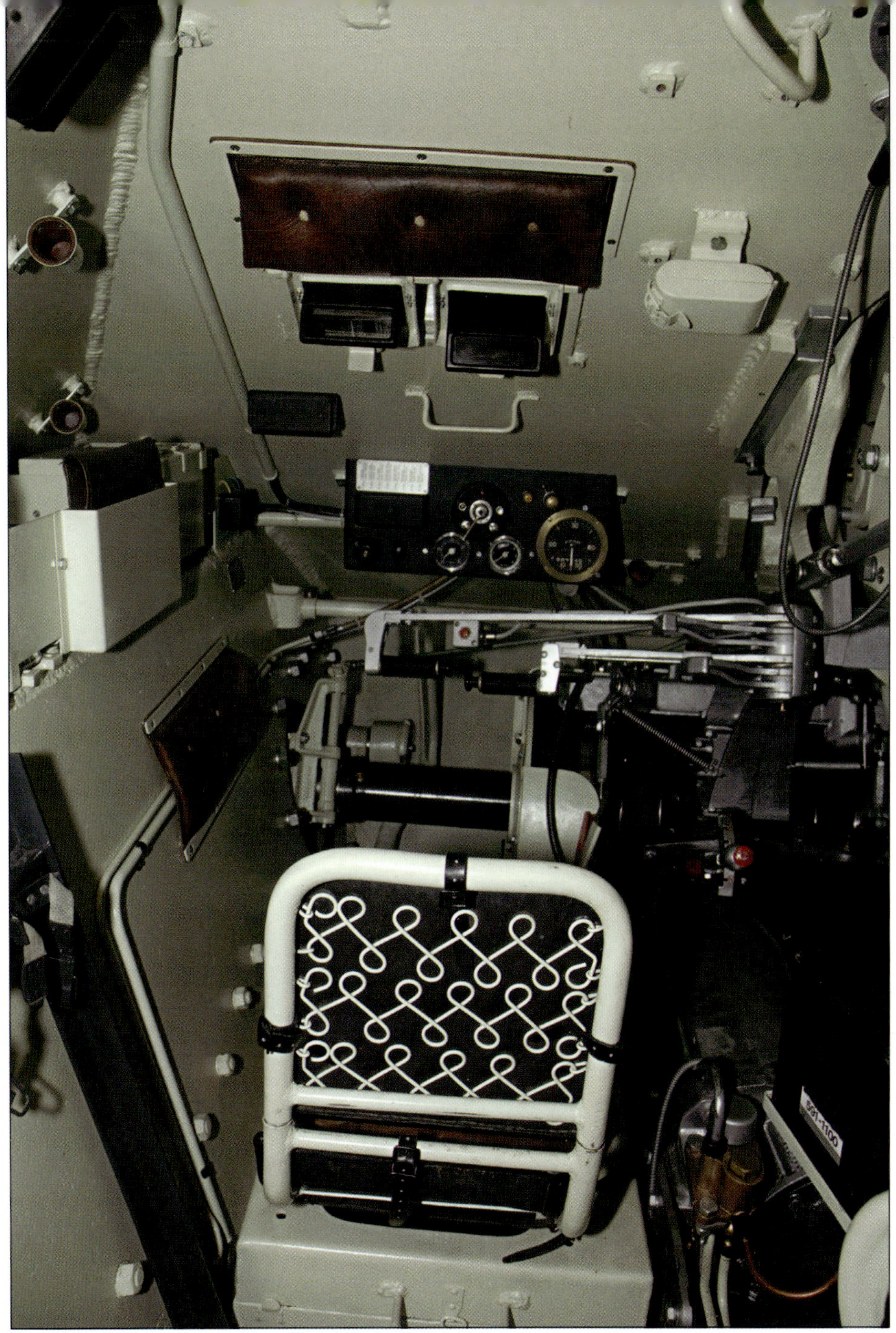

Many components of the Panzerjäger G 13 were taken over from the Jagdpanzer 38, including the periscopes for the driver, the control levers, and the driver's seat. (Walter Hodel)

This Panzerjäger G 13 still carries the small original leather cushion that was a direct take over from the German Jagdpanzer 38. Most G 13s were retrofitted during the course of their service with a larger leather cushion. The two periscopes were mounted in a staggered position, a direct take over from the Jagdpanzer 38. (Walter Hodel)

The layout of the instrument panel was altered on the G 13 – however the size of the panel remained the same as on the Jagdpanzer 38. On the Jagdpanzer 38 the instrument for the radiator's water temperature was located at the far left of the panel. Beside the instrument for the radiator's temperature is the engine revolution counter and on the right is the tachometer. Inside the tachometer is a mileage indicator. The starter switch is located above the instrument on the G 13, this switch was mounted at a low position on the Jagdpanzer 38. (Walter Hodel)

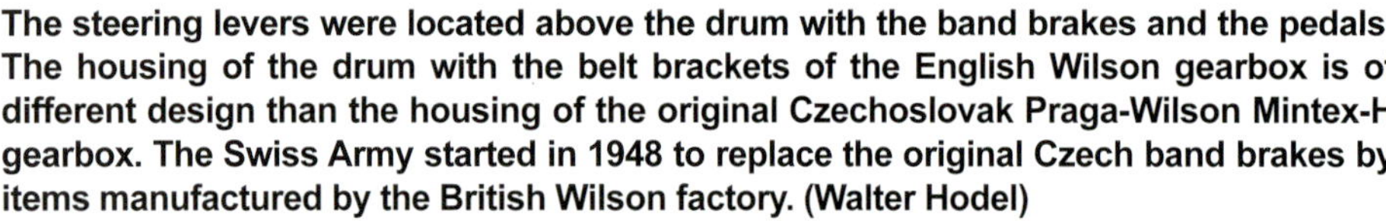

The steering levers were located above the drum with the band brakes and the pedals. The housing of the drum with the belt brackets of the English Wilson gearbox is of different design than the housing of the original Czechoslovak Praga-Wilson Mintex-H gearbox. The Swiss Army started in 1948 to replace the original Czech band brakes by items manufactured by the British Wilson factory. (Walter Hodel)

The pedals for the clutch shift (left), the throttle (center) and the brake (right) are located on the floor of the crew compartment. These pedals were a direct take over from the Jagdpanzer 38. (Walter Hodel)

The steering levers of the Panzerjäger G 13 were a direct take over from the Jagdpanzer 38. The red button is for the driver's intercom, a modification introduced by the Swiss Army in the mid-1950s. Since the driver could not take his hands off the steering levers, communication via headset was done by touching this button. (Walter Hodel)

An upper bracket for the Sturmgewehr 57 (Stgw 57) assault rifle is located on the roof of the crew compartment of the Swiss Panzerjäger G 13. This bracket was introduced around 1960 when the Stgw 57 became the principal assault rifle of the Swiss Army. Previously, the crew were armed only with pistols. (Walter Hodel)

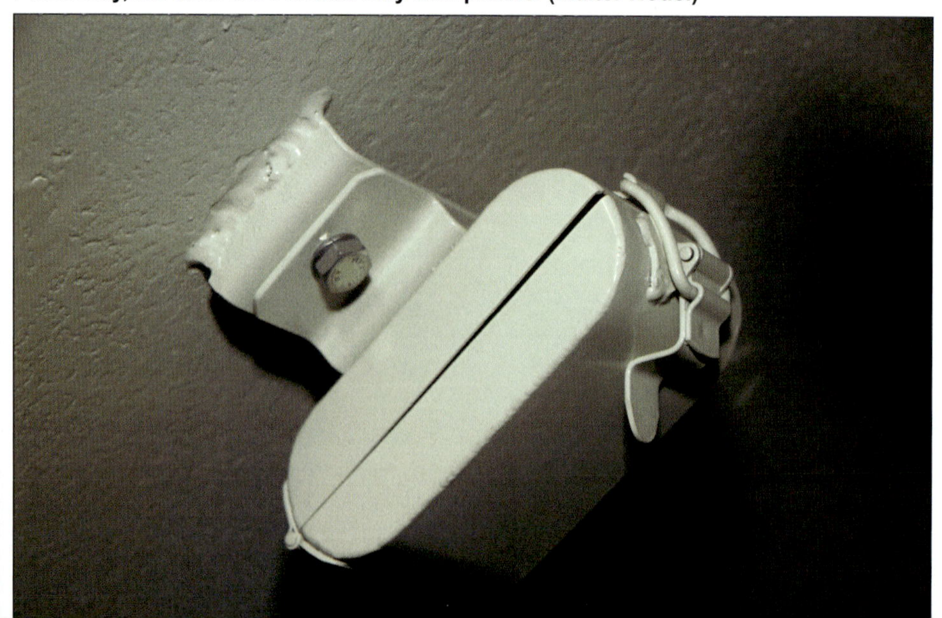

The Sfl ZF1a gunsight mounted in the G 13 was operated by the gunner. (Walter Hodel)

The pannier racks for the ammunition boxes of the Swiss Panzerjäger G 13 were located in a console in the left crew compartment, just beside the driver. The Swiss Panzerjäger G 13 had an ammunition supply of 40 7.5cm grenades, five fewer than late-production German Jagdpanzer 38 Hetzer vehicles carried. The pannier racks were painted in ivory as most of the interior of the G 13.

This plug-in box for the intercom system for the driver and loader is located on the upper left of the crew compartment, just above the driver. (Walter Hodel)

An inboard lamp is mounted on top of the left crew compartment of the Panzerjäger G 13. The lamp served the driver and was one of the modifications introduced by the Swiss Army. No lamp for the driver was ever mounted in the wartime German Jagdpanzer 38. (Walter Hodel)

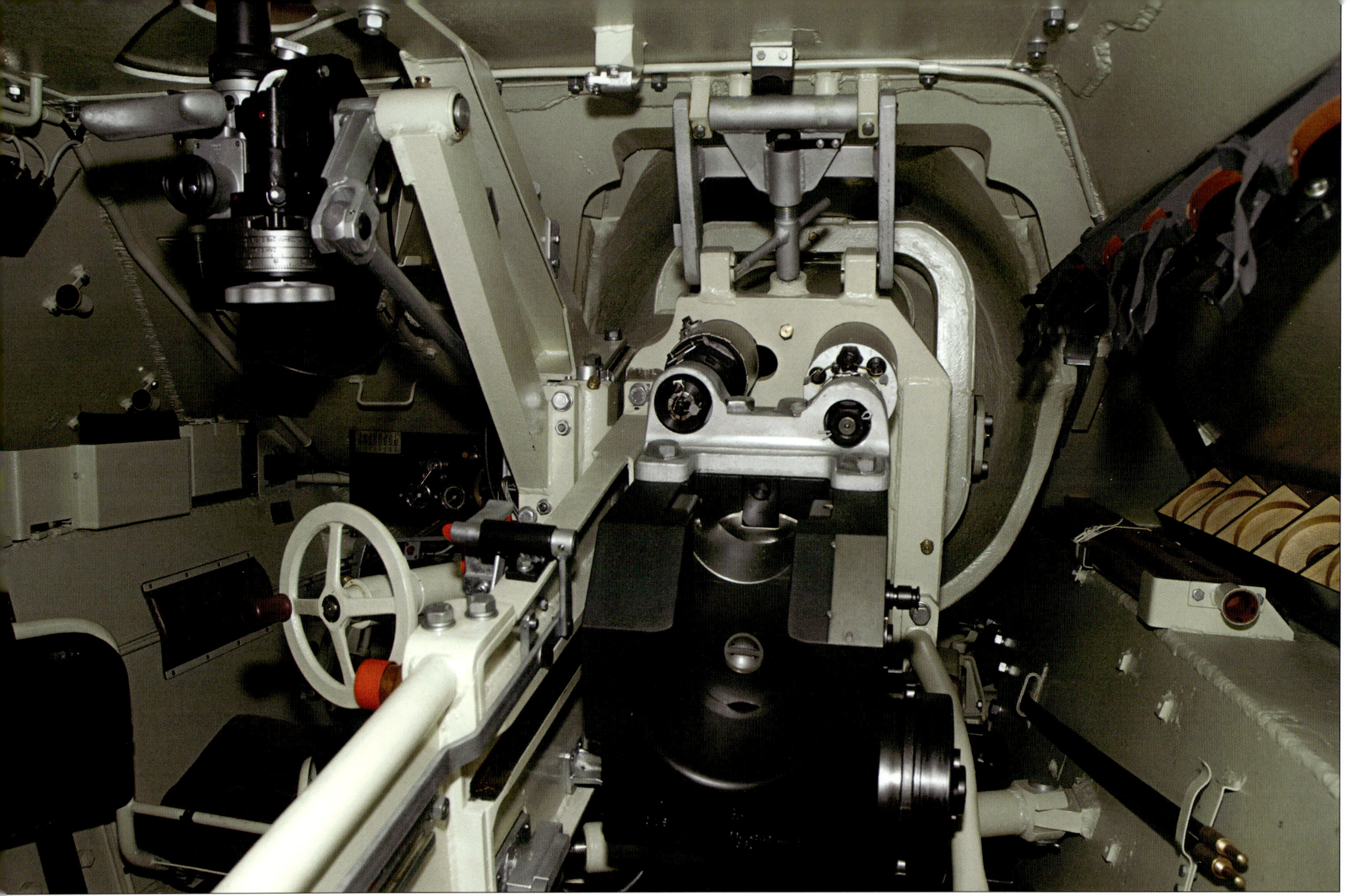

The Sturmkanone 40 (StuK 40) 7.5cm gun used in the Panzerjäger G 13, was manufactured during World War II by Škoda at Plzeň and was available in large quantities after the war. For this reason the derivative of the Hetzer was offered to the Swiss Army with this type of gun. By contrast, the Pak 39 L/48, which had been mounted in the Jagdpanzer 38, was in short supply in Czechoslovakia. The StuK 40 previously saw service in the Sturmgeschütz III assault gun. The sprocket handle regulated the elevation of the StuK 40 7.5cm gun. The Sfl ZF1a gunsight is located on the ceiling. The lock located between the roof and the gun fixed the StuK 40 in position, when the vehicle was in motion. The Panzerjäger G 13 initially adopted the crew positions from the German Jagdpanzer 38. However, the positions for the commander and the loader/radio operator were changed during 1949. On this particular G 13 (hull number 32) the StuK 40 (serial number 45135) was mounted at the Škoda factory at Plzeň. (Walter Hodel)

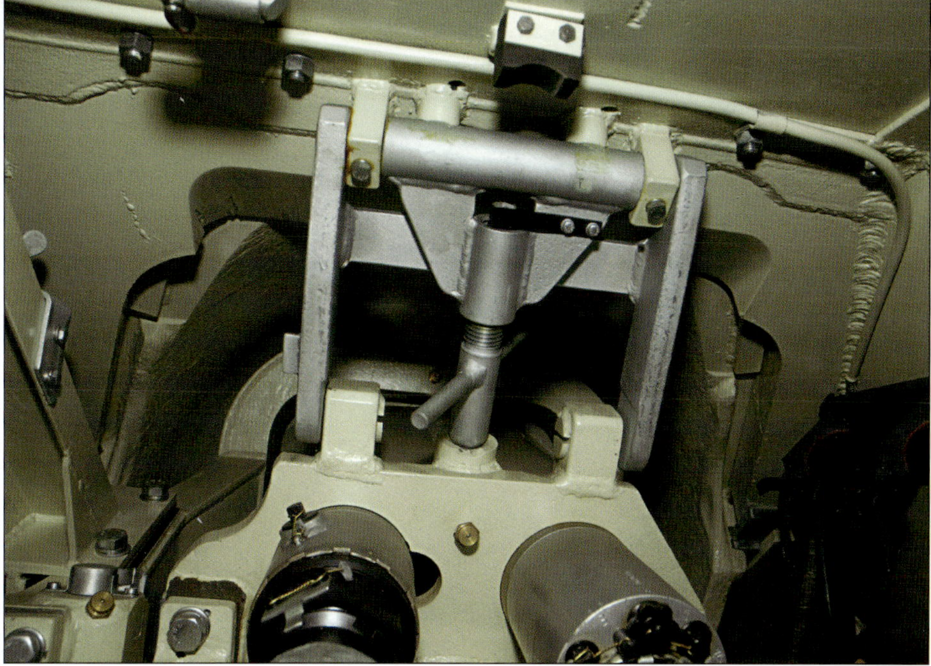

The internal gun travel lock was activated on the StuK 40 when the Panzerjäger G 13 was in motion. This device protected the teeth in the elevation and traversing mechanism from wear during hauls. (Walter Hodel)

The red gun firing button of the StuK 40 gun is located on the left frame of the recoil guard. The firing bottom were made of plastic and a Swiss modification. (Walter Hodel)

The small wheel regulates the traversing of the Sturmkanone 40 7.5cm assault gun. The design of the traversing mechanismn of the StuK 40 was different from the design of the Hetzer's Pak 39 L /48 gun. (Walter Hodel)

The sprocket wheel sets the elevation of the StuK 40 gun mounted in the Swiss Panzerjäger G 13. These sprocket wheels of the StuK 40 were shaped differently from the sprocket wheels mounted on the Rheinmetall-Borsig Pak 39 L/48 anti tank gun of wartime Jagdpanzer 38 Hetzer. (Walter Hodel)

The gunner's periscope and the machine gun gunsight were mounted in the armored ceiling of the left crew compartment of the G 13. The remote operation box for the Swiss SE-202 radio set, manufactured by the Brown Boveri company, was located on the superstructure. Below were the pannier racks for the 7.5cm ammunition. (Walter Hodel)

The rear wall of the crew compartment of a Swiss Panzerjäger G 13 shows the cardan drive shaft and the seat for the gunner. A tube shaped cover protects the shaft. (Walter Hodel)

The crew compartment heating inlet is located on the rear wall of the crew compartment and is a direct take over from the late production variants of the German Jagdpanzer 38. Crew compartment heating was installed for the first time in a German Hetzer in November 1944. (Walter Hodel)

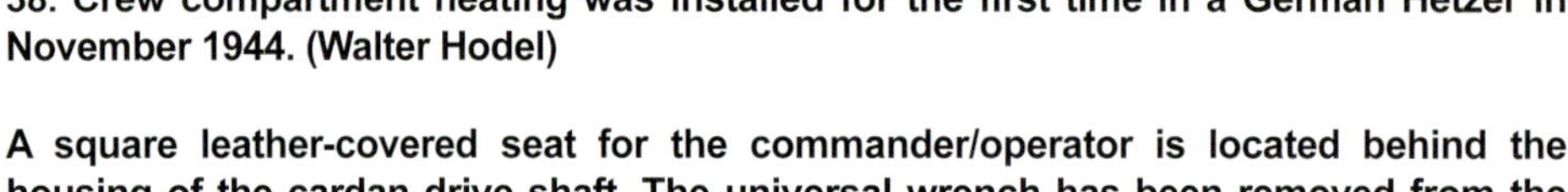

A square leather-covered seat for the commander/operator is located behind the housing of the cardan drive shaft. The universal wrench has been removed from the upper circular frame of the housing and only two screws holding the clip for the wrench remain. (Walter Hodel)

The gunner's periscope is located in the left roof of the crew compartment. The periscope is a direct take over from the Jagdpanzer 38. (Walter Hodel)

The priming pump for fuel and oil of the Swiss Panzerjäger G 13 was located on the rear crew compartment wall and was protected by a covering. There were a number of wartime Jagdpanzer 38 Hetzer vehicles that lacked the covering located above the priming pump. The priming pump for fuel and oil serviced the Praga AC 2800 powerplant that was located behind the crew compartment. (Walter Hodel)

The pannier racks for the 7.5cm ammunition are located beside the circular seat for the gunner. The seat was adjustable in height. There were a total of three pannier racks mounted on the left crew compartment. (Walter Hodel)

A dedicated feature of the Swiss G 13 was the oval shaped escape hatch cut into the 8mm amor plate located on the floor. This escape hatch was a Swiss modification introduced on all 158 G 13s after their arrival in Switzerland. All wartime German Jagdpanzer 38 lacked such an escape hatch. (Walter Hodel)

The hatches on the roof of the G 13 were located on the same position on the German Jagdpanzer 38. (Walter Hodel)

An armor hoop protected the Sfl ZF1a gun sight of the Swiss Panzerjäger G 13. The gunsight as well the armor hoop were a direct take over from the German Jagdpanzer 38 Hetzer and were therefore identical on both type of vehicles. The Sfl ZF1a had an angle of view of eight degrees with a three times magnification. (Walter Hodel)

The arresting mechanism of the crew's right main entrance hatch is seen here. (Walter Hodel)

A distinctive feature of the Swiss G 13 is the armored cupola, mounted on the roof of the tank destroyer. The Swiss Army did not operate the remotely controlled MG 34 machine gun as it did the German Wehrmacht. However, the gun sight for the MG 34 was still retained and covered by this cupola. (Walter Hodel)

The Flab Mg 38 7.5mm anti aircraft gun mounted on the rear engine bay access armor doors was introduced in 1954. This modification resulted in a redesign of the muffler and the relocation of the exhaust pipe leading into the engine compartment.

The rear attachment of the Flab Mg 38 anti-aircraft gun mounted on the Swiss Panzerjäger G 13 was fixed on an U-shaped platform fixed on the upper rear armor plate. The Flab Mg 38 had a rate of fire of 1,200 rounds per minute and was developed from the Flieger Maschinengewehr 29, a hand-held machine gun for aircraft. The Flab Mg 38 was introduced by the Swiss Army for the first time in 1938.

The modified muffler and the rear anti aircraft gun were a unique feature for the Swiss Panzerjäger G 13. Another dedicated Swiss modification was the housing for a drum containing 600 meters of F2-E telephone cable.

The radio operator, who had to lean out of the crew compartment, operated the Flab Mg 38 anti-aircraft gun. No armor shield was provided for the gunner. The Flab Mg 38 used the 7.5mm rounds of the Gewehrpatrone 11 (GP 11), which was the standard ammunition for the Karabiner Modell 1931 and the Sturmgewehr 57: both standard infantry rifles for during the World War II and the Cold War periods.

The engine compartment of the Panzerjäger G 13 was protected by two large armor doors, which were stagged and of different size. An access hatch was located on the left and right base of the armor plate. The arrangement of the armored engine protection doors of the G 13 was a direct take over from the German Jagdpanzer 38. (Walter Hodel)

This is the left engine compartment of a gasoline powered Panzerjäger G 13. The rectangular item is the lead-acid accumulator installed on the left fuel tank box in an insulated container. Beside the accumulator is the circular fuel tank filler located. (Walter Hodel)

The lower engine compartment of the G 13 is viewed through the left access hatch mounted on the lower engine bay cover door. (Walter Hodel)

In the right engine bay of gas-powered Panzerjäger G 13, vehicle M-78039 (hull number 32), is the original Praga AC 2800 engine (serial number 324 837). Mounted on the rear part of the engine compartment is a blowtorch used to heat the engine's coolant water during cold winter operations in Switzerland. (Walter Hodel)

The drum shaped air filters of the Praga AC 2800 engine are located in the right lower engine bay. An oil-soaked element in these filters protected the engine from dust. The ducts of the air filters are connected to the intake necks of the Solex 46 FNVP carburetors. (Walter Hodel)

This is the right engine compartment of a Swiss G 13.

Jagdpanzer 38 "Black 233"

This Jagdpanzer 38, "Black 233," is most unusual as it has totally non-standard idler wheels. The Hetzer is painted in Dunkelgelb RAL 7028 (dark yellow), Olivgrün RAL 6003 (olive green), and Rotbraun RAL 8017 (red brown). The Black Balkenkreuz had a small outline in white. This Jagdpanzer 38 became one of the first vehicles to be captured by the Allied forces on the Western Front.

Jagdpanzer 38 T-038 Hungarian Army

This Jagdpanzer 38 saw action with the Hungarian Army. The Hetzer is painted in Dunkelgelb RAL 7028 (dark yellow), Olivgrün RAL 6003 (olive green), and Rotbraun RAL 8017 (red brown). The Balkenkreuz (beam cross) has been partly overpainted by the registration number of the Hungarian Army.

Jadgpanzer 38 "Chwat"

This early production Jagdpanzer 38 was captured by Polish insurgents during the Warsaw uprising in August 1944. The Hetzer was named Chwat (Daredevil) by the insurgents. The Hetzer is painted in Dunkelgelb RAL 7028 (dark yellow) with an outlining in Rotbraun RAL 8017 (red brown) and Olivgrün 6003 (olive green). This Jagdpanzer 38 previously belonged to the 743. Panzerjäger Abteilung (743rd Tank Destroyer Battalion).

Jagdpanzer 38 “Black 132”

This early Jagdpanzer 38 “Black 132” received Olivgrün RAL 6003 (olive green) and Rotbraun RAL 8017 (red brown) over the original Dunkelgelb RAL 7028 (dark yellow). Jagdpanzer 38 “Black 132” was destroyed in eastern Hungary in autumn 1944.

Jagdpanzer 38 “Black 153”

This Jagdpanzer 38, “Black 153,” previously carried the tactical markings “Red 003.” This Hetzer is camouflaged in Dunkelgelb RAL 7028 (dark yellow), Olivgrün RAL 6003 (olive green), and Rotbraun RAL 8017 (red brown). This Hetzer ended the war in the streets of Prague (Czechoslovakia). Although an early type of Hetzer, it carries the late type muffler configuration.

Jagdpanzer 38 Swiss Army

This Jagdpanzer 38 was briefly evaluated by the Swiss Army in late 1945. This Hetzer received a license plate (M-4086) and a search light as well as a horn mounted on the glacis. Olive drab had been painted over the original German camouflage.

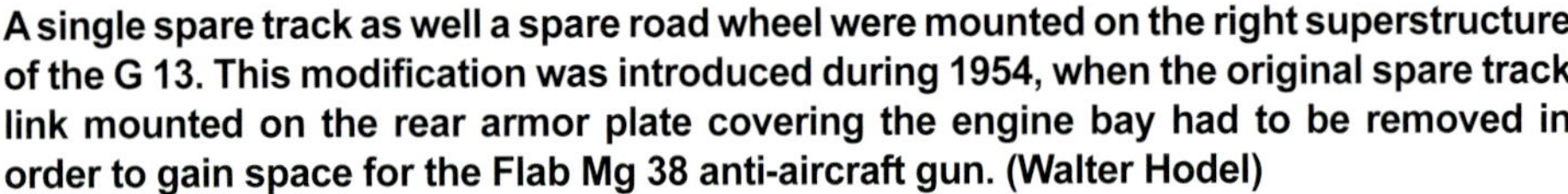

A single spare track as well a spare road wheel were mounted on the right superstructure of the G 13. This modification was introduced during 1954, when the original spare track link mounted on the rear armor plate covering the engine bay had to be removed in order to gain space for the Flab Mg 38 anti-aircraft gun. (Walter Hodel)

The three rows of spare track links were mounted on the left superstructure of the Swiss Panzerjäger G 13. This modification was introduced during 1954 on all 158 G 13 vehcles of the Swiss Army. A boom secured the spare track on the superstructure. These three rows of spare track links was an unique feature of the Swiss G 13s.

The spare road wheel was attached on a support that was welded on the superstructure of the G 13. A metal bar secured the wheel in its position. (Walter Hodel)

The ammunition box for the Flab Mg 38 7.5mm anti-aircraft gun is located on the left superstructure of the G 13. This ammunition box manufactured of sheet metal was a dedicated feature of the Swiss Panzerjäger G 13. The box was mounted on the G 13 during 1954 and held a total of six magazines containing each 100 rounds of GP 11 7.5mm ammunition. All G 13 vehicles had the two horizontally mounted tubular holders for the spare rod antennas deleted shortly after the vehicle's arrival in Switzerland.

A unique feature for the G 13 was the housing for a drum containing a total of 600 meters of drilled F2-E twin telephone cable. This modification was introduced during 1952 on all 158 G 13s of the Swiss Army. The housing was mounted offset to the left of the rear armor plate. This modification enabled the crews to communicate with the infantry units by means of a telephone, which unlike the radio could not be jammed or located by the enemy. Attached to the head of the housing is the Truppenerkennungstafel – a square aluminum plate on which unit marks were inscribed. This square aluminum plate was introduced on all 158 G 13 during 1956.

The rounded diamond-shaped housing for the stop light is of Swiss design and a direct take over from the Panzerwagen 39 (LTL-H) tank purchased by the Czechoslovak enterprise Českomoravská-Kolben-Daněk (ČKD) in 1939. It was equipped with two lights. A stop light as well a rear light for night driving. A few G 13 vehicles had a circular stop light instead of the diamond shaped housing. The rear license plate was painted on the rear armor plate of the G 13. The top corners were always cropped.

The mesh head guard protecting the crew from the hot exhaust gases of the muffler as well the handle welded horizontally on the rear engine bay armor plate, close to the muffler, were both Swiss modifications introduced during 1954. All Swiss G 13 had a straight flame damper, which is a direct take over from the last production batches of the Jagdpanzer 38 built by Škoda at Pilsen in April 1945. Most German Jagdpanzer 38 had the flame damper slanted to the right.

Jagdpanzer 38 "Armin"

Nicknaming armored vehicles was an exception in the German Wehrmacht. The name "Armin" had been painted just in front of the national marking. The Hetzer is camouflaged in an usual pattern of Dunkelgelb RAL 7028 (dark yellow), Olivgrün RAL 6003 (olive green), and Rotbraun RAL 8017 (red brown). This Jagdpanzer 38, which was damaged by Czech combatants in Prague, belonged to the Kampfgruppe Reimann (combat group Reimann).

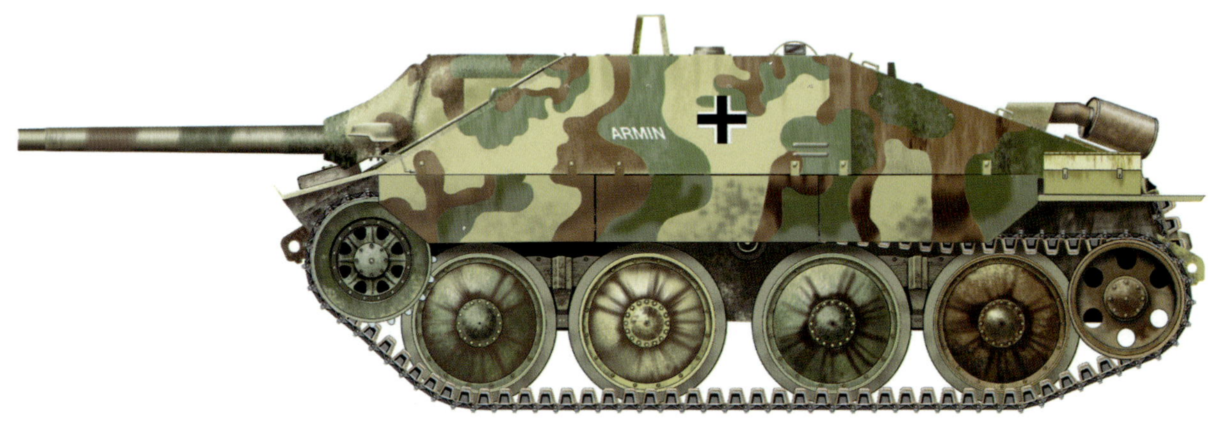

Jagdpanzer 38 "Black 201"

This Jagdpanzer 38, "Black 201," saw action in Bohemia (Czechoslovakia). The Balkenkreuz (beam cross) is outlined in white, but the tactical number is not outlined.

Jagdpanzer 38 "Thule"

This winter-camouflaged Jagdpanzer 38 was named "Thule" by its crew. The Hetzer took part in the defense of Berlin in April 1945 before it fell victim to the Red Army.

Jagdpanzer 38

Many Jagdpanzer 38 vehicles saw action whithout any tactical or national markings. This is a typical pattern applied by the Škoda factory at Plzeň. Hard-edged wavy lines of Olivgrün RAL 6003 (olive green) and Rotbraun RAL 8017 (red brown) were applied over the base coat of Dunkelgelb RAL 7028 (dark yellow).

Jagdpanzer 38 - Halloville

This Jagdpanzer 38 was destroyed by an M10 of the U.S. Army at Halloville, France, in November 1944. This Hetzer has a carefully applied "Licht und Schatten" (ambush scheme), which was applied at the factory. The "Licht und Schatten" camouflage had been applied for the first time in summer 1944. The ambush scheme was painted by hand and was not airbrushed.

Jagdpanzer 38 - Škoda

This Jagdpanzer 38 was produced in April 1945, when a shortage of paint became evident. A pattern of Olivgrün RAL 6003 (olive green) had been applied over the Rot RAL 8012 (red) primer. This Hetzer, built by Škoda at Plzeň, has a white-outlined Balkenkreuz (beam cross), but lacks tactical markings.

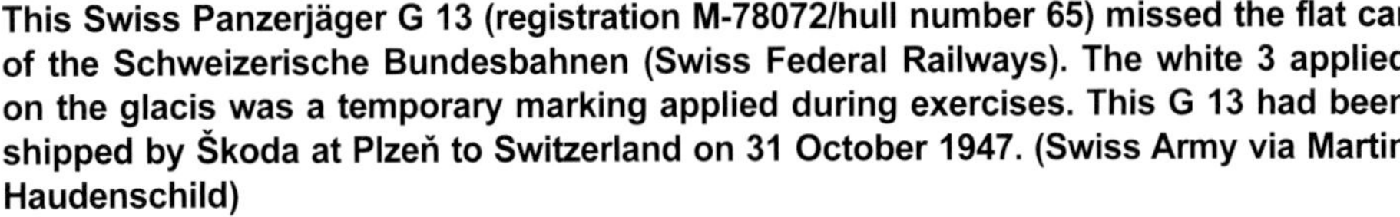

This Swiss Panzerjäger G 13 (registration M-78072/hull number 65) missed the flat car of the Schweizerische Bundesbahnen (Swiss Federal Railways). The white 3 applied on the glacis was a temporary marking applied during exercises. This G 13 had been shipped by Škoda at Plzeň to Switzerland on 31 October 1947. (Swiss Army via Martin Haudenschild)

This G 13 had been carefully camouflaged by its crew, that has parked their tank destroyer in front of a Swiss farm house. The search light has been turned 180 degrees to the rear to avoid a reflecting of the sun in the glass, thereby revealing thei vehicle's position to the opposition forces. A multi color camouflage tent square made of fabric had been draped over the glacis of the G 13. (Swiss Army via Martin Haudenschild)

This Swiss Panzerjäger G 13 has a horizontal muffler taken from a Panzerwagen 39 (LTL-H) tank. The Swiss Army purchased a total of 24 Panzerwagen 39 (LTL-H) tanks from Czechoslovak enterprise Českomoravská-Kolben-Daněk (ČKD) in 1939. Part of the original exhaust stub remained on the vehicle. This type of muffler configuration was not widely used by G 13s in the Swiss Army. The protection skirts were missing on this G 13 during its firing trials. (Swiss Army via Martin Haudenschild)

This Panzerjäger G 13 has the Truppenerkennungstafel – a square shaped plate made of aluminum – attached on the lower left edge of the upper front armor plate, which is not standard. On most G 13 vehicles, this plate was mounted on the upper edge of the lower left front armor plate. A Willys Jeep purchased from U.S. Army World War surplus stock follows the G 13. A single Jeep was assigned to each G 13 in the Swiss tank destroyer formations. (Swiss Army via Martin Haudenschild)

Large white letters were introduced as identification markings on the glacis in 1950 and continued to be applied on the G 13 vehcles until 1958. The G 13 in the foreground is the M-78130 (hull number 143/engine number 324 916), which was accepted by the Swiss Army at Plzeň on 15 October 1948 and was shipped to Switzerland on 30 November 1948. These G 13 vehicles took part in an army parade held at Basel on the Rhine River in July 1951. (Swiss Army via Martin Haudenschild)

With the exception of the first eight vehicles, all G 13s had the license plate painted on the lower right part of the upper armor plate. This G 13 M-78151 (hull number 164/engine number 324 919) lacks the search light. The G 13 M-78151 was shipped from Škoda factory at Plzeň to Switzerland on 16 February 1950 and belonged to the last batch of 20 G 13s delivered to Switzerland. (Swiss Army via Martin Haudenschild)

The crews of four G 13s and a Sherman tank prepare for an exercise at the proving ground of the Swiss Army at Thun. The Sherman was purchased by the Swiss Army from surplus stocks of the US Army after the end of World War II. (Swiss Army via Martin Haudenschild)

This Swiss Panzerjäger G 13 (registration M-78154/hull number 167) has the temporary tactical number 43 applied in yellow on the glacis and the superstructure. The number is repeated on the Truppenerkennungstafel in black. Such individual tactical markings were removed from the tank hunters after the end of the Wiederholungskurs (repetition training course). The search light as well the protection skirts are missing on this vehicle. This G 13 was accepted by the Swiss Army at Plzeň on 8 March 1949 and is now part of the French Armor Museum at Saumur. (Swiss Army via Martin Haudenschild)

A G 13 (registration M-78138/hull number 151) climbs a hill in the Swiss Alps during a Wiederholungskurs (repetition training course) in the early stages of the Cold War. These Wiederholungskurse for tank crews were held each year for a duration of three weeks. The muzzle brake of the StuK 40 (serial number 50181/1022) is protected by a fabric covering, a most common practice during exercises. Traces of the letter "R" remain on the right superstructure of this G 13. A single GMC truck is parked in the background. A total of 500 GMC trucks were purchased from U.S. Army surplus stocks in 1947. The single GMC follows an FBW 4x4 5 ton truck and a Saurer 4x4 3.5 ton truck. The FBW and the Saurer trucks were both developed and manufactured in Switzerland. A number of Swiss manufactured Condor A-580/I motorcycles are parked just beside the Saurer 4x4. Neither a spare road wheel nor a spare track link is mounted on the right superstructure of this particular Panzerjäger G 13, indicating that this picture was taken before 1954. The particular G 13 (M-78138) had been accepted by the Swiss Army at the Škoda factory at Plzeň on 8 March 1949. However, the Communist government of the Czechoslovak Socialist Republic (ČSSR) – under the pressure of the Soviet Union – did not allow the export to Switzerland until 16 February 1950. This G 13 belonged to the last batch of 20 vehicles to be delivered to Switzerland. All Swiss G 13s were camouflaged in dark gray overall at the Škoda factory. The last G 13s were retired in 1973 and were indeed world's last examples of the Jagdpanzer 38 Hetzer derivative to be phased out of service. (Swiss Army via Martin Haudenschild)